THE FILMS OF

ROBERT REDFORD

By James Spada

The Citadel Press   Secaucus, N.J.

ACKNOWLEDGMENTS

Special and heartfelt thanks go out to Robert Chiarello and Chris Nickens for their unending willingness to help, their good humor, their photographs and, most of all, their friendship. Another special debt of gratitude is owed Lois Smith and Robbi Miller of Pickwick Public Relations for all their assistance and courtesies. For their research assistance, thanks to Dick Gingrich and the staffs of the Lincoln Center Library of the Performing Arts and the Academy of Motion Picture Arts and Sciences. For their invaluable recollections, a nod to Sydney Pollack, George Roy Hill, Michael Ritchie, Mike Nichols, Herman Shumlin, William Goldman, Stark Hesseltine, Francis Lettin, Sidney Furie, Robert Mulligan, Gene Saks, Jean Thomas, Monique James, John Saxon, Bill Craver, Conrad Janis, Julie Harris, Mildred Natwick, Natalie Schafer. Others whose help is greatly appreciated are: Lester Glassner, Lou Valentino, George Zeno, Ralph Celentano, Larry Paulette, Dennis Gregory, Roger Morain, Rich Stanley, Bob Suzuki, Rick Sparks, Richard Amsel, Tim Custer, George Nelson, Bill Kenly, Steve Mitchell, Barbara Petty, Madeline Eller, Jim Parish, Vito Russo, Steve and Fran Gurey, Don Stanke, Mel Shestack, Bruce Curtis, Jim Cone, Mike Minor, Ruth Pearce, Madeline Franklin, Mindy Leon, Muriel Mitchell, Marjorie Marting, Ron deArmond, Maria Segal, Charles Stumpf, Bruce Siegel, Eileen DiBartolomeo, Fran Coniglio, Rebecca Armstrong, Vicki Botner. Broadway photos by Joe Abeles. TV photos courtesy the broadcasting networks, movie stills courtesy the producing photos from *The Way We Were* by Robert Chiarello.

Dedicated to
MEL SHESTACK
O selfless man and stainless gentleman!
ALFRED, LORD TENNYSON
The Idylls of the King—Merlin and Vivien

First paperbound printing, 1978

Library of Congress Cataloging
in Publication Data
Spada, James.
 The films of Robert Redford.
1. Redford, Robert. 2. Moving-picture
actors and actresses—United
States—Biography. I. Title.
PN2287.R283S6   791.43′028′0924 [B] ·76-13161
ISBN 0-8065-0654-7

Designed by LESTER GLASSNER

CONTENTS

FOREWORD

Shortly after he completed filming *All the President's Men* in April 1976, Robert Redford was offered $2 million by producer Joseph E. Levine to appear in his new film, *A Bridge Too Far*. Redford's role was to be a small one that would take just two weeks of his time to film.

This, perhaps better than anything else, illustrates the position of pre-eminence held by Robert Redford in the motion picture industry today. *The* male sex symbol of the seventies, he consistently wins popularity polls and heads box office lists, usually along with Barbra Streisand, his female counterpart in prominence. Redford—in the tradition of Hollywood leading men of the past—is a reflection of the American tastes of the time he lives in: the glorification of the blond, California Golden Boy image, the accent on easy-going sexuality, the desire for "cool." But rather than being a reaction to the dark, brooding "rebels" of the fifties and sixties, Redford is a blend of the glamorous leading men of the past and the independent, intelligent, concerned young man of today.

Robert Redford never wanted to be an actor. He spent years preparing for a career as an artist, and got into acting not only accidentally but practically against his will. He worries that acting is unmanly and unimportant, and has often indicated that he doesn't very much enjoy what he does for a living. And yet, in a paradox inexplicable even to him, Redford is one of the hardest-working, most dedicated actors around. He has made seven movies in the last four years, and his latest, *All the President's Men,* occupied two solid years of his time, as he took part in every business and creative aspect of the filmmaking.

Redford's life and career has been a series of fascinating contradictions. Born in California, the dream capital of the world, goodlooking and a star high school athlete, Redford was unhappy and discontent, considering his life empty and worthless. Once he became an actor, he took roles as sadistic killers to avoid pretty boy stereotyping; after making his first movie he walked out on a contract and didn't work in films for another three years. He took roles others were avoiding just for the challenge; he thought often of quitting. But in spite of Redford's independence and unorthodoxy—or perhaps because of it—he became one of the biggest stars in Hollywood history.

In this book, by recounting this complex man's life and career through his own recollections and those of the people closest to him, I have tried to paint as complete a picture as possible of the person and the actor who is Robert Redford. But I doubt that anyone can fully understand Redford. He is an incomplete man—a man who will try many more things in his attempt to be a total human being. There are several more books left in Redford. This one is only a start.

James Spada
Los Angeles, California
November, 1976

BOB REDFORD

California's Van Nuys High, from which
Redford graduated in 1955

PART ONE

Growing Up Redford

Charles Robert Redford, Jr. was born on August 18, 1937, the only child of Charles and Martha (Hart) Redford. The Redford family made its home in Santa Monica, California, not far from the American Dream capital of Hollywood where, most of America was convinced, life was always beautiful and everyone was always happy. But life wasn't that beautiful for the Redfords.

Mr. Redford worked long hours as a milkman, then as an accountant. "He was gone in the morning when I went to school and in the afternoon when I came home," says Bob, "so I felt like I never saw him. But even in the rough times, I never wanted for anything. He was always working so hard."

After World War II, things got better financially for the Redfords. Mr. Redford became an accountant for Standard Oil, and the family moved from Santa Monica to the middle-class area of Van Nuys. Young Redford's family life was solid. "My mother was a good woman, a joyous person who found the positive in everything. She was full of life. Both my parents were very straight. They believed in sacrificing for the children. They were terrific, very loving."

But his parents' sacrifices caused young Redford some disquiet: "They were part of the ethic of the Fifties; you work hard and sacrifice for your kids, so they better toe the line. 'I'm working so you can have such and such . . .' Guilt! And do I hate guilt!"

By the time Bob reached adolescence, he was unhappy with life in California, unhappy with school, unhappy with the times he lived in. "The Fifties had no personality," he says. "As teenagers we had nothing to identify with. And nothing originated from the generation I was in. We didn't project anything of our own. We just took what was given to us secondhand, changed it a little bit and went on. It was boring and maddening, and it bothered me. I wanted out of it."

Redford had no great love for Van Nuys, either. "It was a cultural mud sea. No excitement, no romance, no edge, no nothing. Just a dull thud. The schools were primitive. You sat in your little rows with your little inkwells and pledged allegiance to the flag and bells rang to let you in and out. I hated it."

And he rebelled against it. He rarely got good grades, rarely listened to what the teacher was saying. He would sketch classmates rather than participate in the day's work. He forged report cards and did a lot of daydreaming. School never challenged him; his native intelligence and curiosity couldn't be stimulated by books. "I prefer learning from actual experience."

One of his first portrait sittings: age 4

Posing for his yearbook with fellow classmates

To fight the boredom he felt in his existence, Bob created his own brand of excitement—often, in the process, getting into trouble. He and his best boyhood friend, William Coomber, wreaked their own brand of havoc.

"We used to do things like climbing buildings around Hollywood," Redford says. "And towers. The Fox Village Theatre and the Bank of America were our favorites. We thought that was the pinnacle of our lives at the time—climbing towers and unscrewing lightbulbs from the signs and throwing them down."

Some of the high jinks were a little more serious. Redford recalls stealing hubcaps and "selling them to a fence for $20 apiece." Once, with "a bunch of guys in a hot-rod club," Redford broke into Universal studios and "broke a lot of stuff." He'd look at fancy houses and think, "What have *they* done to deserve all this?" The young Redford was fascinated with wealth. "I was always trying to wrangle an invitation to a rich friend's house."

At fifteen, Bob and his buddies were active, strong, athletic, all-American boys. They thought actors were sissies. "We used to sneak into movies and then make fun of the actors, yelling things like 'You tell her, lover boy!' at the screen." But Bob and Bill Coomber decided there was *one* masculine activity for a man in the movies—stunt work. And they decided they could do it as well as the guys they were seeing at the local picture show. "So we went to Warner Bros. and, miraculously, we got in to see the casting director. We told him we were stunt men wanting work. He was very, very polite; asked our ages, what experience we had, took our names and addresses and said that at the present he had nothing for us, but would notify us when he needed stunt men. Of course, we never heard from him."

If Robert Redford at this time in his life had a passion, it was sports. He excelled at tennis, swimming, baseball and football. "I was good at sports. I did it so much because it was easy." Redford's abilities made him a star high school athlete, and sports consumed the greater part of his teenage life.

Young Redford also "had a lot of girl friends," but he was never happy with the way his youthful milieu dictated women be treated. "The high school jock could always get the girl," Redford remembers. "We used to just cruise down the street in our cars, pull up alongside a girl and say nothing but 'get in.' As a group, we never treated girls like people."

But there were some romantic moments when he was alone with girls. "When I had a date, I wouldn't take her to drive-ins like the other guys. Instead, we'd take off for the beach and explore."

When he was eighteen, Bob's mother died. Reluctant to talk about it now, he'll only say, "I was hit hard." His mother's death caused him to think deeply about his life, and what he saw didn't please him at all. "I felt less of an obligation to stick around," he says. To get away, he accepted a baseball scholarship to the University of Colorado. The school appealed to him because it was far from California and close to mountains for climbing and skiing.

At first, he made a real effort to succeed. "I worked to get good grades just to prove I could." He even joined a fraternity. But before long, the dissatisfactions of his youth began to nag Redford more and more. "I couldn't learn anything in school. And I got tired of the one-dimensional life of the athlete. It was just a constant, terribly tiresome round of practice and steaks. I never knew what it was like to just enjoy a sport. I was always out there grovelling to win. You begin to fear not winning. One day I realized how narrow my life had been, that I disliked the system that produces test-tube athletes."

Redford started skipping baseball practice, usually for drinking sessions. His inattention to the game lost him his baseball scholarship, and he soon flunked out. "It was the beginning of a three-year period when it seems I was drunk every other day," he says. "I don't remember much of 1956."

Redford started drifting back and forth across the country, taking odd jobs to support himself. "I would always discover something new or meet someone interesting. My real education I got on the road."

By now Bob was getting deeply involved in art, and his sketching gave way to painting. His art courses at college were the only ones that kept his interest. If he had a goal in life at this point, it was to be an artist. After his drifting brought him to New York City, he decided to study art in Europe.

He bummed around the continent for several months, hitchhiking and living in youth hostels in Greece, Germany and Paris. His existence, to say the least, was meager. "I would go through the market area in Paris and cadge carrots and vegetables to eat. Sometimes I'd go to Harry's Bar, where Americans used to hang out. If you hung around long enough, somebody would buy you a meal."

In France, Redford was determined to fit in. "I tried to dress and look like a Parisian. I got a sketch book, wore a beret I stole in New York and sat around Montmartre sketching, generally looking like a fool. An American tourist took thirty-four camera shots of me until he discovered for himself I wasn't really a French sidewalk artist. What tipped him off to my real identity were Argyle socks. He was furious when he noticed them."

At one point Redford got involved in some student demonstrations in Paris. "I thought of myself as a revolutionary," he says. "I got clubbed by policemen who didn't know I was just someone from Van Nuys. It didn't radicalize me; it sobered me up. I realized I didn't know what I was doing there. I was just hungering for action."

Bob moved on to Italy, where he began seriously to study art in Florence. But it was there that his life's frustrations, confusions and disillusionments began to take their toll. "I was living in a very, very small room. I had only one outfit and I wore it constantly. I spent a lot of time alone—I mean, *really* alone. I went long periods without eating, mostly because I didn't have the money, but I enjoyed the fasting. I was

At 15, Redford was one of the stars of the Van Nuys High tennis team . . . and a member of the Art Club.

11

A few members of the Van Nuys Tennis Team

willfully putting myself into a bleak situation."

Redford would spend nights in his room, drinking and smoking cigarettes. "So much was happening to me mentally that I couldn't handle it. I thought that the professor I admired most was rejecting my painting, and it was a terrific blow." Redford began thinking about death. At times, he would concentrate on a small part of his room for hours until he began to hallucinate. He started to conjure up physical symptoms of madness and sickness and began to see strange creatures. "It was exciting," he says, "but then it got frightening because I felt I was losing control of it. And it certainly wasn't anything I could share with anybody. I didn't feel like any of my friends could understand."

Redford's feelings of inadequacy as an artist weren't helping his situation. His favorite professor, after Redford unveiled a painting he was particularly proud of, told him, "You're not making any progress. You're just imitating."

Disillusioned and "messed up," Redford left Italy and started to hitchhike wherever a ride would take him. Nothing seemed to matter to him. He had no desire to go home. He just wanted to move.

After a while, for lack of anything better to do, Redford did return home to Los Angeles. His life there wasn't much better. "I felt like I'd aged and become an old man. No one could relate to what I'd been through at all, and so it went back inside me, and I started drinking worse than ever because I didn't have anybody to share that experience with. "I was just dying a little bit each day. Heading right downhill, and almost enjoying it. The worse it got, the more I kind of liked it. I really didn't have the energy to come out of it. I might have gone under in some way."

What pulled him out of it was meeting a young woman named Lola von Wegenen. In a short time, she was to help Redford pick himself up and turn his life around. "I remember the first time I ever saw Bob," says Lola. "It was 1958 and we both lived in the same building in L.A. He was sitting on a brick wall, barefooted, wearing jeans and a vest— with nothing under it. I thought he was the greatest thing I'd ever seen."

The feeling was mutual. "I needed to talk to someone who could understand what I'd been through," says Bob, "and Lola's attitude was fresh and responsive. She was genuinely interested in what I had to say, at a time when I really needed to talk."

The couple would spend hours together walking the streets of Hollywood, talking until dawn. But, as Lola remembers it, they never really "dated" until several months had passed. "Our relationship got off to a better start because we were honest with each other. All that stuff that comes from dating wasn't there. When you date, you want a guy to think you're neat, so your true personality doesn't come out until the third or fourth time because you're trying to be 'nice.' And you don't get to know each other because you're so busy doing your numbers. Bob and I just talked our way into love."

Lola helped Bob gain a new perspective on his life and he decided to continue to study art, at New York's Pratt Institute. But Lola couldn't accompany Bob to New York. It was another year before they were married.

At Pratt, Bob thought it might be interesting to learn about theatrical scenic design. A friend suggested that if he were serious about getting into theatre, Redford should study acting to learn about the stage and make the right contacts, and suggested the American Academy of Dramatic Arts. Redford wasn't sure. "The trouble was, I never liked actors. But I didn't really give a damn, so I went to audition." He was too ashamed to practice in his room, so he went to Central Park to learn his lines.

He was required to deliver two passages, one comic, one tragic. "The teacher made me mad," he says. "I started to read the comic monologue and it was utter disaster. But during the second one, I just looked at the man and got angrier. I was supposed to be telling someone off, so it worked out pretty well."

The entire admissions committee, including the man who incurred Redford's wrath, was impressed. He got an "A" on the audition, and the committee members compared him in their notes to Spencer Tracy. Although they agreed he would have to discard his California accent and learn how to project his voice, they thought he had "a natural ease of expression, good imagination and flair."

One of Redford's high school yearbook illustrations

Still, Redford held back for a long time. "I went into acting pre-disposed against the life, and it took a long time to get down through all the muck and all the hang-ups. I hated the Academy until one day in movement class, we had to put choreography to a poem. I was damned if I was going to. But the teacher kept calling on me, and I finally got up without even thinking and went right into *The Raven*, the only poem I knew by heart, and I used the entire room. I was all over it, flipping and twisting, running out into the hall, grabbing people out of their chairs. I got to the end and the teacher said, 'Fine, now do it again.' And I did it again! I was suddenly so free I could do *anything!*"

It was an opinion shared by most of his instructors. Their quarterly reports on his progress contained nothing but praise. "Excellent stage presence. He's learning an actor's discipline. He should develop into a very fine talent," wrote one instructor. Despite Redford's own feelings that he was lazy, another instructor wrote, "He's hard-working, creative, responds well to direction, shows fine promise, thoughtful interpretation of character." A third said, "Leading man material. Excellent sense of use of feelings. Impressive ability and potential, especially considering complete lack of experience."

One of the most perceptive comments by Redford's instructors at this time was that "acting is important to him, even though he may hide it with a certain nonchalance."

Francis Letton, one of Redford's instructors, recalls that Redford's interests at this time were more toward American works such as *Bus Stop* and *A Streetcar Named Desire* than to classical theater. "I remember once he saw an announcement casting him in Chekhov's *The Seagull*, and he wasn't happy about it at all. One of his classmates, Ron Liebman (who later co-starred with him in *The Hot Rock*) said, 'That's a great part.' Redford just looked at him and said, 'I never heard of it.' "

As it turned out, three of the four plays Redford did while at the Academy were classical. "His talent," says Lettin, "warranted putting him in material beyond the kind of stuff he would have preferred doing. He was a little puzzled by it at the time, but he came back to the Academy recently and told the students he realizes now that that was one of the greatest compliments he ever had, being put into that kind of work."

One of his classical performances was as Creon in *Antigone*, and Lettin remembers being very impressed. In his notes on the show Lettin wrote, "I believe that Bob has a very big talent. He has grace of movement, courage. Seems full of a deep anger, and uses it constructively. Has an appreciation of beauty—an awareness of ugliness—and is not afraid of either. Has quick personal identification. I feel he has an expression of freedom and should not be pinned down—yet."

Lettin firmly believes Redford is one of the finest actors in America

Art teacher Jean Doobrova supervises Redford and his fellow Yearbook Art Staff members

today, but he admits most people don't think of Redford as a great actor. "I think it's because the public tends to think of actors generally as being flamboyant," he says. "Bob is very much like Spencer Tracy, who's also a graduate of the school, in that he deals with the reality of a character, the reality of human behavior, what people *do*. There's a certain subtlety in that, of course, that the layman doesn't see. But people did grow to accept Tracy as one of the finest actors there was in this country. Bob's still relatively young in the profession, and he's just not a flamboyant person."

Redford insists that he wasn't taught how to act at the Academy. But he admits he did come away with something. "The Academy taught me that you can only be as good as you dare to be bad. I learned not to be afraid to do things in front of people. They called it 'stepping outside of yourself.' They had a lot of clever terms for things like that. It was a question of taking whatever was there and bringing it out. It wasn't really learning. The best thing an actor has is his instincts, and I don't think you can learn them. I've worked with actors who've studied with Strasberg and stuff and they're mechanical people. They work technically off of a formula that I don't think works very well. I don't think you can technicalize acting. At the Academy I got the space and the opportunity to expand and form myself as an actor but I didn't learn how to act. Acting being institutionalized academically is a turnoff to me. I really wasn't happy in the school." Nevertheless, Redford's thoughts about theatrical design faded as he became more deeply involved in the acting world.

As he looked while studying at the American Academy of Dramatic Art

While studying at the Academy, Bob kept in touch with Lola through letters and phone calls. Finally, the separation became too hard to bear and Bob called Lola and proposed over the long distance telephone. After several days of thinking about it, she accepted, and Bob went back to California, where they were married in September of 1958. "When we got married," says Lola, "it was almost like marrying a hippie for a 'li'l ol' Mormon girl' to marry an actor. He was exactly the type of boy my parents had warned me not to go out with."

The newlyweds hitchhiked back to New York, where they lived in a walk-up on Columbus Avenue in the Eighties. With Bob studying full time at the Academy, Lola worked at a bank to provide financial support. They didn't have much money. They exchanged their wedding gifts for cash. Their furniture was largely whittled by Bob, and Lola's homebaked bread became the staple of their diet. But it wasn't to be long before their furnishings and their diet improved.

PART TWO

Redford on Broadway

After two years of study at the Academy, Redford got a chance to make his Broadway stage debut. One of his instructors, Mike Thoma, was also the stage manager of the Broadway hit *Tall Story*. The show's director, Herman Shumlin, asked Mike if he could round up some of his students to replace several actors in a crowd scene. As Shumlin recalls it, "A group of basketball players were protesting the suspension of the star player because of bad grades. All we needed were buys who looked like high school students and could dribble a basketball."

Redford didn't hesitate a minute when asked to audition. "I threw on a sweater to make me look younger, and ran right down." The audition consisted of nothing more than dribbling a ball across the stage. Although basketball was the one sport Redford never played in high school, he was able to fake it well enough to get the part.

Although one of many and with just a single line—"Hey, they're in here!"—Redford made an impression on Shumlin. "He stuck in my mind because he had an excellent stage presence. He was extremely believable."

Another individual who felt this way about Redford was Stark Hesseltine, a theatrical agent. Stark first saw Redford when Thoma, a friend, sneaked him into an Academy performance. Agents weren't allowed to see students before their graduation because the school was afraid they would pirate them away. Although Redford had just a small part in a party scene, Hesseltine was very impressed. "He never opened his mouth, but I saw such a presence, such a look of concentration, that I literally couldn't take my eyes off him."

Thoma told Hesseltine "hands off" until Redford graduated. Seeing him again as Creon in *Antigone* ("It was an incredible performance. I had to have him!"), Hesseltine called Redford to his office at MCA as soon as his AADA studies were complete. He discovered a very independent, skeptical young man.

"He sat there and challenged me to convince him that he needed an agent."

Hesseltine convinced him, and Redford was now a represented actor. Before long, Stark was sent the script of *The Highest Tree* by Dore Schary. He submitted Redford's name and Bob auditioned for the casting director Ruth Frankenstein. "After he read," says Hesseltine, "he stood in Shubert Alley waiting for her decision." It was favorable.

The play concerned a nuclear physicist, played by Kenneth McKenna, who learns he has six months to live and attempts to rectify some of the evils of his profession's experimentation with nuclear blasts.

Redford's was a small role, requiring perhaps six lines of dialogue. He played Natalie Schafer's son and Elizabeth Ashley's brother. (Later, he would co-star as Ashley's husband in *Barefoot in the Park*. "It was," he says, "kind of like incest.") Then, Ashley was known as Elizabeth Cole.

The play wasn't an entirely pleasant experience for Redford. Natalie Schafer remembers that Dore Schary, the play's director as well as author, wasn't too impressed with Bob. "Besides," says Natalie, "Schary wasn't really a director. It was hard on Bob, as inexperienced as he was, because the direction was pretty weak. Everyone in the cast thought it was Bob's very first show, because he was so nervous. Schary kept harping on him about his projection and certain aspects of his performance. It made Bob very insecure. He wasn't sure enough of himself at that point to argue."

During the show's out-of-town tryouts, Bob and Lola's first child was born. They named him Scott. Within two months, however, their joy turned to tragedy—the child succumbed to the mysterious, unexpected "crib death." It was a shattering experience. Bob took a few days off and the entire company took up a collection for them, because, as Natalie Schafer puts it, "They had so little money in those days." The couple went on a long weekend drive

One of Redford's earliest publicity photos

As Frederick Ashe, Jr. (Buzz) in *Highest Tree*

Rehearsing *The Highest Tree* with Kenneth McKenna

through Pennsylvania to be alone with their sorrow and take stock of their lives. Within a few days, Bob was back with the play and giving it his all.

The show opened in New York on November 4, 1959 to mixed—mostly negative—reviews. It lasted just twenty-one performances. "From instinct I thought the play was pretty bad," says Redford. "On opening night the cast was getting wires and messages connected with the play, all reading 'good luck to a wonderful guy' or 'to a swell fellow, nice having you with us in the company,' etc. None of them mentioned anything about being a good actor.

"I was told I must go to Sardi's afterward because that's what people do. I was embraced by people on the street and by the time I got to the restaurant I was convinced I'd been wrong and that it must be a great show. The party was very gay; then someone came in with the papers and the critics said it was a bomb. I'd ordered a turkey sandwich and by the time it arrived the crowd had disappeared. I figured I'd better eat because I'd probably have to go on rationing after all these glad hands slunk away."

After *The Highest Tree* closed, Redford got no offers of further work. Needing money, he took off for California and did ten TV dramas, several of which brought him high critical acclaim. In the fall of 1960, he returned to New York for an important Broadway role, opposite Julie Harris in *Little Moon of Alban*, a drama by James Costigan which had originally been presented on TV.

The play concerns a nurse (Julie Harris) during the Irish Revolution whose lover (Robert Redford) is killed by a British soldier. Later, through an unusual set of circumstances, she finds herself caring for—and falling in love with—the very man who killed her lover.

The show's director was Herman Shumlin, who hadn't forgotten the impression Redford made on him in *Tall Story.* "After his audition," says Shumlin, "I insisted that he be given the role." Shumlin was even more impressed with Redford once *Alban* rehearsals began. "He had impeccable acting taste and was totally believable in the part. Once I told him, 'I think you can be what Spencer Tracy was in theater. When Tracy walked on stage, the theater disappeared, he was so entirely in possession of the stage. I think you have that same quality.' Redford just stared at me." But Shumlin saw a major flaw in Redford's performance. "I told him that whenever he had a scene with Harris, he wasn't allowing himself the higher level of performance which I knew he was capable of. It seemed he was too much in awe of Julie's stature. They were never equal in their scenes together."

Julie Harris saw this as a problem as well. "He did seem to be in awe of me. I'm supposed to be this monument or something. It's really quite ridiculous to be in awe of anything. Redford was very timid. I thought to myself, 'He's an actor and he must know we're supposed to be lovers.' But I was getting no response. So I overdid the affection, figuring that way he'd get the point. But there was always this wall between us."

Redford remembers the whole thing quite different-ly. "It's true I was somewhat in awe of her," he says, "but being in awe of someone has never stopped me from working well with them. What created the wall between Julie and me—and I'll never forget it, it was the most extraordinary thing—was that on the first day, she came into the rehearsal without a script. She had the part down cold. I like to stay loose and allow things to happen, allow characterizations to grow and relationships to evolve onstage. But her responses were all set in cement. There wasn't any room for any chemical interaction between us. The lines were all worked out, the moves were all worked out, the emotions were all set from the first day. There was nowhere to go. It was intimidating to me because

Left and above: Rehearsing *Little Moon of Alban* with Julie Harris

Stefan Gierasch, Redford and Liam
Clancy rehearse their roles as Irish
Republicans

this was only my second speaking role on Broadway
and it was a big deal for me.''

As impressed as Shumlin says he was with Redford,
Julie Harris recalls that he gave Bob "a hard time.
Shumlin is a very stern director. He used to tell
Redford incredible things like, 'No, I want you to
hold your hand like this'—minute details most
directors hardly bother with. He never did anything
like that with me. Maybe it was because Redford was
so new.''

"I had a difficult time early in my career because I
got angry very easily," says Redford. "I didn't like to
be told—I've always hated being overdirected. I don't
respond to it at all. I remember not thinking much of
Shumlin as a director, thinking he was old-fashioned.''

Redford as Dennis Walsh and
Julie Harris as Brigid Mary
Mangan

Rehearsing *Sunday in New York* with Pat Stanley

With Pat Harrington, Sr., Pat Stanley and Sondra Lee during rehearsals

While *Little Moon of Alban* was in Washington on its way to Broadway in November of 1960, Lola gave birth to a girl whom the Redfords named Shauna. "I insisted he be allowed to go up to New York to see his new daughter," says Julie. "So for a few days his stand-in did the part."

Little Moon opened in New York on December 1, 1960 and Redford received his first notices. all of them good. But the show was not a success and closed after only twenty performances.

Following another stint in Hollywood, where he did some more TV work and made his first film, *War Hunt*, Redford asked his agents to find a comedy for him to do on Broadway. He wanted to get away from the heavy drama he'd been doing on television, but his agents weren't sure it was the right move. "They told me no, I shouldn't do comedy. That was a whole other ballgame," says Redford. They told him it required special training and style to pull off. "That sounded like nonsense to me. Acting is acting. So I pressed them to find a comedy I could at least read for."

They came up with *Sunday in New York*, about a newspaperman's romantic involvement with a zany young woman to be played by Pat Stanley. David Merrick was producing and Garson Kanin directing. Merrick also felt that Redford wasn't right for the part. "He's a fine dramatic actor," Merrick told Redford's agents, "but this requires a light comedy touch." After much cajoling, Merrick agreed to hear Redford read, but added, "I won't pay his way from California to read because I don't think he's right." Redford paid his own way back to New York.

Meeting with Redford before he was set to read, Garson Kanin told him he reminded him of Spencer Tracy, a good friend. "You even resemble him, when he was younger. Are you sure you're not related?"

"I think that may have helped convince him to give me the part, because after two readings I got it," says Redford. "And an interesting footnote to all this is that Merrick never did reimburse me for that airplane ticket from California."

Several bizarre events occured during the show's tryout in Washington. One day, in the middle of a seduction scene between Bob and Pat Stanley, 150 people in the audience picked themselves up and walked out. "Needless to say," relates Conrad Janis, the show's third lead, "there was quite a commotion, and Bob and Pat were trying to figure out what was happening and play the scene as well." The group, it turned out, was from a local Catholic girl's school and their group leader had no idea of the subject matter of *Sunday in New York*. Once she found out she made her girls leave.

Another time, a water heater caught fire after Pat Stanley had plugged it in during a scene. Bob, Pat and Conrad attempted to put the fire out, all the time

ad-libbing jokes in the pretense that it was part of the script. The audience caught on, however, and once the fire was extinguished, burst into applause. "As usual," says Janis, "Redford remained completely unflappable."

Once the show opened in New York on November 29, 1961, things went pretty smoothly--except when Redford decided otherwise. One April Fool's Day, he decided it was time to play a good joke on Stark Hesseltine. "I used to get disgusted with an audience that gets up and puts its coats on and turns its back on you when you're taking your bows," says Redford. "Stark was constantly afraid I was going to do something wild because I have a short temper. So I got Lola in on it."

She called Stark and said, "I don't know how to tell you this, but . . . did you hear what happened?"

Hesseltine went white and shouted, "What happened? WHAT?" "W-w-well," Lola whimpered, "It's Bob. He's in jail. Last night he stepped across the footlights and slugged somebody—and they're pressing charges. And there's another thing he did . . ."

On cue, Lola hung up on that note of certain horror. And, as per Bob's instructions, she didn't answer when Stark frantically called back. Once enough time had passed to insure that Stark would go crazy with anxiety, Lola called back and said, "There's another thing I have to tell you—April Fool!"

Sunday in New York was not a big success. The reviews were mixed, although Redford received excellent notices. Howard Taubman of *The New York Times* exclaimed, "Mr. Redford has personal charm; he will be a matinee idol if he doesn't watch out."

Although the show closed after just a few months, Redford's career was shifting into a higher gear. If he was disappointed that his first Broadway efforts were less than successful, he wasn't discouraged. He would be back.

In October of 1962, playwright Neil Simon and Broadway producer Saint Subber met to discuss the production of Simon's latest comedy *Barefoot in the Park*, about the marriage of a stuffy Wall Street lawyer to a free-wheeling, off-beat girl and their resultant problems. They had a leading lady, Elizabeth Ashley, and had decided to ask Mike Nichols to direct. They hadn't decided on a leading man.

Nichols read the play and liked it, but he had a condition before agreeing to direct. "I told them that if I could have the man I'd seen on TV the night before play the lead, I'd do the show. The man was Redford, the TV show was *The Voice of Charlie Pont*, and I remember Redford was remarkable in it. He had great authority and was extremely interesting. It was immediately apparent that he was an unusual actor." Simon wasn't sure who Redford was, but Saint Subber and Elizabeth Ashley had been impressed by his

work in *Sunday in New York* and all soon agreed to hire Redford.

On the first day of rehearsal, several of the people involved with the play wondered whether Redford had been the right choice. "After we had done a few scenes," says Nichols, "the stage manager and some others were saying that the girl was good and Mildred Natwick was wonderful but they were a little worried about Redford, because he seemed so quiet. I told them to give him time. He wasn't performing for them, he was working on the character. I knew he'd be fine in the part."

Redford recalls he wasn't at all sure he wanted to do the show. "I just didn't want to be there. At the time, I was out in Utah, building my house. I stayed with it until three-thirty in the morning before catching a six-thirty plane to New York for rehearsals. And then I was back and they were all talking so fast and it was all about the theater, and it seemed so unreal to me—AshleydidafilmandthisonewasinsummerstockandNicholsgotmarriedyatatayatat—and I was thinking *I built a house.* I couldn't get those rocks out of my head. And I was lousy in the part, really bad. I just couldn't get with it, and I wanted to quit, but Nichols wouldn't let me. He took me to dinner during tryouts and said, 'I know you want out, and I know what the problem is. I can't explain it to you but I know what it is. And I'm not letting you out. You can go to Broadway and be lousy—worse than you are here—and I won't fire you. So make up your mind.'"

"I wasn't aware of any lack of concentration on Redford's part," says Nichols, who remembers the details differently. "The problem was that Elizabeth Ashley was playing to the audience and getting a big response from them. Audiences are often drawn to a pretty girl, and she was in her slip most of the time, and the part was flashy. Redford, on the other hand, was truthfully and honorably playing his part, relating only to Ashley and the other actors, and he started to disappear on stage.

"So I had dinner with him. I had had experience with this problem before because I had a girl partner when I was half of the comedy team. I told him, 'You can't win a battle until you acknowledge that there is a battle going on. And whenever two people are on stage, friends and colleagues though they may be, there is a kind of subterranean battle going on for the attention of the audience.' And I told him that he knew what I knew—that if he wanted to, he could wipe up the stage with Ashley. And that in order to do that he had to admit there was a contest—which he would then win with one hand tied behind his back.

"And I remember it vividly because that night he very slightly and almost invisibly increased the *size* of what he was doing. He didn't play up to the audience,

because I don't think his pride would permit it and someone with his talent doesn't have to do that anyway. And just that slight alteration on the performance made a spectacular difference—that night you couldn't even *see* Ashley on the stage, it was all Redford. As the weeks progressed, we balanced it out, and we never had that problem again."

Redford regrets that his professional differences with Ashley were carried over into the press as a full-blown, bitter feud. "It was never true. It was overwrought. I really liked her. Subsequent to that, I understand that she read a piece or somebody told her something that blew it all out of shape or misquoted me or something, saying I spoke badly of her. Then I heard she was on a TV show talking about it and saying how hurt she was that I had been so ratty and said these terrible things. She was obviously very bitter about it, and I wanted to write her a letter and then I thought, No, that just doesn't do any good.

"But I feel badly that all this has come about. I liked her—there was something very sympathetic about her, even with all her harshness and bravura." Ashley herself admits that she wasn't easy to work with because of severe personal problems. "I was already in analysis, but I just couldn't connect. At twenty-four.I had become a raging schizoid. All the frustration I had inside me I turned on the people around me. Neil Simon was incredibly kind to me, and believe me, I wasn't an easy girl to be kind to. Robert Redford and Mildred Natwick . . . I was bitchy to both of them. I can't ever make it up to them, but I hope they understood."

On the whole, however, Redford's experience with *Barefoot* was a pleasant one. He wasn't especially fond of the character he played, stuffy Wall Street lawyer Paul Bratter, because his personality was so alien to Redford. But Nichols recalls that Bob got a perverse enjoyment out of the character. "He played the part with a tremendous lack of vanity. Bratter was rather square, and Redford took great pleasure in plastering his hair down and wearing a little box coat with a velvet collar and pressing his tie in the dictionary and all the semi-prissy things that were part of the character."

There was a terrific *esprit de corps* among the cast members as well. Bob became especially friendly with Mildred Natwick and Herb Edelman. It became a sport to try to make Bob break up on stage. Mildred Natwick would mutter wisecracks to Bob as the audience laughed at one of the show's lines. In one scene, Bratter is suppose to be drunk, and as he opens a door and says something to his wife, it comes out garbled, making him laugh at his drunken state. The cast took to doing strange things outside the door to see if they could get Bob to crack up for real. "It started to escalate," remembers Bill Craver, the com-

Rehearsing *Barefoot in the Park* with Elizabeth Ashley

A publicity shot for *Barefoot*

The cast: Elizabeth Ashley, Redford,
Kurt Kaszner, Mildred Natwick

pany manager, "and it just started to be one bizarre thing after another." On Bob's birthday, Liz Ashley hired a stripper who stood naked in the doorway as Bob opened it, Craver recalls. "He laughed so long it disrupted the play. It got so he would open that door with a combination of expectancy and apprehension."

One night Redford turned the tables on Mildred Natwick. "I love Mildred's quiet dignity," says Bob. "She had a chauffered limousine pick her up after the performance each night and deliver her home. On her birthday I cancelled this service without telling her and had a hansom cab there instead with a driver in full regalia."

Redford had arranged for Herb Edelman to step out in front of the theater with his foil just as Bob was putting her in the carriage and they fenced. Bob grabbed Mildred by the waist and cried, "Into the carriage, Milady!" A mob collected, the horse started rearing and off they went with a lurch. "She was a bit scared at first," says Redford, "but soon came out of her shell, waved to the people and called 'Hello, everybody—it's my birthday!'

"We went through Central Park," says Mildred, "and Bob stood up waving his sword. From the opposite direction came another coach with a young couple in each other's arms. As they passed, Bob brandished his sword and cried. 'Unhand that girl!' I'm sure they were startled, to say the least."

The crews' good times, of course, were made possible by the show's phenomenal success. It was an immediate smash, the lines so long for tickets the week after it opened that the management supplied coffee and donuts to the standees. Once Redford realized the show would run for a while, he sent for Lola and the children to come to New York.

Redford wasn't used to long Broadway runs, and he began to get bored with performing the same script every night. He admits he's only good for about two and a half months. After that, his perversity came out in *Barefoot*. "I created accidents and problems to break the monotony. If you came out with one shoe off one night, at least it made life happen on stage. Otherwise, it got pretty stiff after a while."

Although the show ran for four years, Redford bowed out of the cast less than a year after the opening, on September 5, 1964. He was replaced by Robert Reed. It marked the last time he has appeared on a stage. Explaining why, he says, "There was a revolution in the New York theatre at the time of *Barefoot*. It was really the twilight of the romantic sex comedy. The commercial aspects were drowning the theatre's good qualities. I was looking for something with some literary quality and there wasn't anything for me in that revolution. Nothing has come along in the theater since then that has interested me enough to attract me."

So Redford abandoned the stage in favor of movies.

THE HIGHEST TREE

CAST

Aaron Cornish, Kenneth MacKenna; *Isabel,* Miriam Goldina; *Dr. Robert Leigh,* William Prince; *Susan Ashe,* Natalie Schafer; *Frederick Ashe,* Howard St. John; *Frederick Ashe, Jr. (Buzz),* Robert Redford; *Steven Cornish,* Frank Milan; *Caleb Cornish,* Richard Anderson; *Amy Cornish,* Gloria Hoye; *Mary Macready,* Diana Douglas; *Bronislau Partos,* Joe De Santis; *Jane Ashe,* Elizabeth Cole; *Arkady Clark,* Robert Ritterbusch; *John Devereaux,* Larry Gates; *Gloria Cornish,* Shirley Smith.

CREDITS

Staged, Directed and Written: Dore Schary; *Settings and Lighting:* Donald Oenslager; *Costumes:* Marvin Reiss; *Associate Producer:* Walter Reilly; *Production Manager:* Jean Barrere; *Stage Manager:* Arthur Marlowe; *Press Representative:* Nat Dorfman; *Produced by the Theatre Guild and Dory Schary at the Longacre Theatre. Opened November 4, 1959.*

REVIEWS

"*The Highest Tree* lacks sensational theatrical impact, but it is a provocative and arresting drama... Kenneth MacKenna, returning to the stage after twenty-five years, plays the scientist with understanding, flexibility and, when the script calls for it, dramatic intensity. The supporting cast is consistently competent..."

> WATERS,
> *Variety*

"Dore Schary has penned the most urgent and provocative drama of the season . . . At last, we have a playwright who tackles contemporary themes with courage, taste and intelligence . . . The cast is superbly directed by the playwright himself . . .It is a pleasure to watch actors who do not tear up the scenery to make their points. But the evening quite properly belongs to playwright Schary. Hurrah!"

> *CUE*

"Mr. Schary could easily have gained our admiration for a brave attempt to dramatize a subject to which only a great playwright could do justice . . . but a dramatized essay which at its end reveals that its author has no charges to make or no new insights to offer is downright maddening."

> HENRY HEWES,
> *Saturday Review*

The cast in a party scene (Elizabeth Ashley is with Natalie Schafer)

"A message play? Yes, *The Highest Tree* is a message play. But don't be frightened by that. Go, instead, and listen to what Dore Schary is saying in a quiet voice, in unmistakable words. So excellent a craftsman is he that he has been able to put his dynamic thinking in human terms which are completely understandable. It's a fine play which is short of greatness only because of the number of things Mr. Schary must say. Considered as an evening of theater, this has everything. There is a gripping story and there are fine performances of well-drawn characters. Kenneth MacKenna is at once deeply moving and very impressive. Nearly matching him in magnitude is Diana Douglas . . . Other good performances are Robert Redford as the nephew, Gloria Haye, Elizabeth Cole, Miriam Goldina and Shirley Smith."

ALTA MALONEY,
Boston Traveler

31

Posing with the cast of *Highest Tree*
during rehearsals. Left to right: Redford,
Howard St. John, Barbara Loden (later
replaced by Elizabeth Ashley), Kenneth
MacKenna, Richard Anderson, Natalie
Schafer, Gloria Hoye and Frank Milan

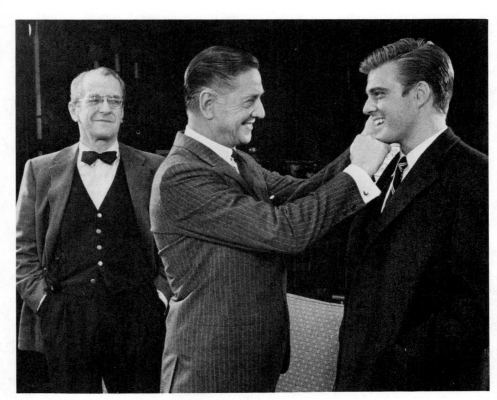

With Kenneth MacKenna and Frank Milan

With Kenneth MacKenna

LITTLE MOON OF ALBAN

CAST

(In Order of Appearance)
Dennis Walsh, Robert Redford; *Patch Keegan*, Stefan Gierasch; *Tom Phinney*, Liam Clancy; *Sergeant Reynolds*, Norman Barrs; *Shelagh Mangan*, Nora O'Mahony; *Brigid Mary Mangan*, Julie Harris; *Lt. Kenneth Boyd*, John Justin; *Father Curran*, Neil Fitzgerald; *Sister Servant*, Barbara O'Neil; *Sister Catherine*, Mary Ann Hoxworth; *Sister Barbara*, Joyce Sullivan; *Sister Theresa*, Helena Carroll; *Sister Angelica*, Susan McClintock; *Sister Martha Kevin*, Beulah Garrick; *British Soldier*, Scott Middleton; *Bertie*, Roger Hamilton; *Sergeant Peale*, Jamie Ross; *Pvt. Wigan*, Michael Lewis; *Doctor Clive*, Eric Christmas; *Black and Tan*, Roy Pritchard; *Convalescent Soldier*, James Duncan; *Sister Marie Louise*, Sadie McCollum.

CREDITS

Presented: Mildred Freed Alberg; *Directed:* Herman Shumlin; *Written:* James Costigan; *Lighting and Setting:* Jo Mielziner; *Costumes:* Noel Taylor; *Opened December 1, 1960 at the Longacre Theatre.*

REVIEWS

"*Little Moon of Alban* as a television drama seemed a beautiful love story about a wounded British officer and the little Irish nurse who makes him care enough about living to fight against imminent death. On the close-up medium of TV we watched in fascination the subtle interchanges between Lieutenant Kenneth Boyd (played remarkably by Christopher Plummer) and Brigid Mary Mangan (enacted radiantly by Julie Harris). In expanding *Little Moon of Alban* for the stage, however, Mr. Costigan has chosen to supply a great deal more for the background to his story, with the result that instead of seeing the Irish Revolution through its impact on the lovers, we tend to see the lovers as one of a number of the Revolution's casualties . . .Dennis Walsh (is) portrayed with boyish charm by Mr. Redford."

HENRY HEWES,
Saturday Review

"It is left to Miss Harris to imbue the play with what radiance it attains . . .In a series of soaring vignettes, Miss Harris makes visible what Mr. Costigan leaves blurred . . . She is playing all women who love men, hate war and live in agony that war makes a mockery of their love. She is completely the mistress of the tragedy's every mood. Surrounding this portrait of a modern Deirdre are a number of bright fragments of acting. The most nearly matching is that of John Justin . . .and, more briefly, that of Robert Redford as the shining, sacrificial young Irishman."

JAY CARMODY,
Washington Evening Star

"Julie Harris gives an exquisitely touching performance . . . Robert Redford is admirable as the sweetheart . . . Devotees of O'Casey, J.M. Synge and W.B. Yeats will probably find *Little Moon of Alban* exciting and satisfying, but it may be forbidding and too special for the general public."

WATERS,
Variety

"The actors serves as a wonderful backdrop for Miss Harris. John Justin is more than a backdrop. O'Neil, Robert Redford, Nora O'Mahony, Helena Carroll, Stefan Gierasch, Liam Clancy, Eric Christmas and the others help considerably . . ."

EMORY LEWIS,
Cue

"The two stars are ably abetted by Robert Redford, as the susceptible and patriotic Irish lad who is one of the sacrificial victims of the strife . . ."

THOMAS R. DASH,
Women's Wear Daily

"There is a splendid performance by Robert Redford in the brief role of the slain Irish Republican . . ."

RICHARD WATTS,
New York Post

"Robert Redford emerges as a winning and attractive young actor. Unhappily, he is done away with too soon . . ."

NEWSDAY

Brigid Mary Mangan and Father Curran comfort a dying
Dennis Walsh (with Julie Harris and Neil Fitzgerald)

With Julie Harris and Nora O'Mahoney

With Pat Stanley

As Mike Mitchell

SUNDAY IN NEW YORK

CAST

(In Order of Appearance)
Adam Taylor, Conrad Janis; *Eileen Taylor,* Pat Stanley; *Man,* Pat Harrington, Sr.; *Woman,* Sondra Lee; *Mike Mitchell,* Robert Redford; *Russell Wilson,* Ron Nicholas.

CREDITS

Presented: David Merrick; *Directed:* Garson Kanin; *Written:* Norman Krasna; *Settings and Lighting:* David Hays; *Costumes:* Patricia Zipprodt; *Assistant Director:* Russell McCraig; *Choreographic Consultant,* Tilda Morse. *Opened November 29, 1961 at the Cort Theatre.*

With Pat Harrington, Sr., Ron Nicholas,
Conrad Janis, Pat Stanley and Sondra Lee

With Sondra Lee

REVIEWS

"*Sunday in New York* is, like almost all American comedies about sex, concerned with who might have been sleeping with whom (but wasn't), who may be sleeping with whom (but isn't) and who, after much salacious hinting about, will be sleeping with whom once there is no more need to ask for whom the wedding bell tolls. This farce is not exactly a comedy, except in the first act, where some feeble pretense is made at dealing with people and their problems, such as what is a single girl to do in face of the standard American male's double standard about virginity.

"Swinging on the creepers of this writhing jungle is a quartet of acrobatic comedians performing monkeyshines in virtuoso fashion. Robert Redford, as an amiable part-time critic on the make, is winning, witty and enormously resourceful; he now proves that the comic mask fits him as snugly as the tragic one always did, and enters the tiny band of young actors who are as versatile as they are prepossessing."

Theatre Arts

"Actors Stanley and Redford pump fresh air into Krasna's soggy script, especially its laugh-shy first act. But they cannot camouflage the fact that this type of play has long been outgrown by just about everyone whose first love was not a box office."

Time

"Sandy-haired Robert Redford is a marvelously skilled farceur as the stranger."

RICHARD L. COE,
Washington Post

"Norman Krasna is the cleverest word acrobat of the season. He has taken a dull, routine Broadway comedy subject (virginity—will she or won't she?), and turned it into a droll and diverting comedy . . .Garson Kanin has staged the sex game with enormous wit and imaginative details . . .The sextet of actors is a casting call dream. Pat Stanley . . . is not only attractive, she is in her first straight dramatic role, a most deft comedienne. Sondra Lee, a pint-sized Christmas package, is a gifted sprite. . . Robert Redford, Ron Nicholas and Conrad Janis are great assets, too."

Cue

"There are engaging performances by Miss Pat Stanley and Robert Redford. . . These two have the right attitude toward extravagant comedy. They maintain a delightful air of innocence . . ."

JOHN CHAPMAN,
New York Daily News

"Appealing Robert Redford, who is really first-rate no matter what the evening is doing, can dart in and out of an all-too-evident bedroom, begin to lash his tie around his neck without having a shirt to go under it, listen with his own private radar to the confusing under-currents that keep changing the room temperature, and finally propose solving the whole dilemma by a mass lie (if everybody lies to a man, how can that man possibly continue to believe the evidence of his own eyes?) with a bland bafflement that is always precisely triggered."

WALTER KERR,
New York Herald Tribune

As Paul Bratter

BAREFOOT IN THE PARK

CAST

(In Order of Appearance)
Corie Bratter, Elizabeth Ashley; *Telephone Man*, Herbert Edelman; *Delivery Man*, Joseph Keating; *Paul Bratter*, Robert Redford; *Mrs. Banks*, Mildred Natwick; *Victor Velasco*, Kurt Kasznar.

CREDITS

Presented: Saint Subber; *Directed:* Mike Nichols; *Written:* Neil Simon; *Setting:* Oliver Smith; *Lighting:* Jean Rosenthal; *Costumes:* Donald Brooks. *Opened October 23, 1963 at the Biltmore Theatre.*

With Elizabeth Ashley

With Mildred Natwick after ascending the stairs

With Mildred Natwick

REVIEWS

With Kurt Kaszner, Mildred Natwick, Elizabeth Ashley

"This felicitous, fey frolic is as lighthearted, airy and gay as a Sunday bike ride in Wall Street or kite-flying in Central Park. One laugh gracefully somersaults over another in the risible romp. The plot? There isn't one, really . . . Its charm is in its bittersweet wit, its insouciance, its contemporaneity, its very special Manhattan flavors. Mildred Natwick. Kurt Kasznar, Elizabeth Ashley and Robert Redford constitute the basic foursome. They are all utterly accomplished."

Cue

". . . Director Mike Nichols has added a breathless busyness of his own. But Mr. Nichols doesn't busy his actors for the sake of motion alone: if Mr. Redford comes charging across stage muffled to the mouth like one of those little Italian statues of Winter, it's because, at these temperatures, exercise is important; if Mr. Redford makes a furious dash toward upstage left, it's because he's going to put his tie in the big dictionary for pressing, and who could question so urgent a need?"

WALTER KERR,
New York Herald Tribune

"Let's call it 'cute.' . . . A little sluggish here and there, perhaps, and certainly not a side-splitter, but funny, light and well-played . . . Mr. Redford is a 'great big lug' type and, if not very charming, is pro-fessional."

MARTIN GOTTFRIED,
Women's Wear Daily

"Well, welcome *Barefoot in the Park* to the ranks of dull hits. It is a play with all the mannerisms of comedy that yet manages to be funny only intermit-tently. It has been directed and is performed with a glassy smoothness that frees the playwright from the need to write punchlines: the spectators can see what's coming when the character merely opens his mouth, and they obligingly laugh on cue. It is peopled not by characters but by the generalizations of characters in funnier plays . . . It is entirely second hand, entirely crass, and for those of us who imagine the theater with some relevance to life (even in its breeziest humor), it is obscene."

Village Voice

PART THREE

Redford on Television

Robert Redford's television apprenticeship lasted longer than those of most Hollywood stars of his stature. He appeared in over thirty dramas between 1960 and 1964, playing a variety of roles and often generating a good deal of excitement about his characterizations.

The first Redford TV vehicle to gain him widespread attention was the last *Playhouse 90*, a stark drama entitled *In The Presence of Mine Enemies*. Monique James, then his agent at MCA, recalls it wasn't all that easy to land Redford the part.

"I represented a fellow who was just getting hot named George Peppard. The *Playhouse 90* people called me and said they wanted him for the role of the young Nazi soldier. I read the script and thought that George was too old and really not right for the part."

Monique called Ethel Wynant, the casting director of *Playhouse 90* to say that George Peppard declined the part. Then, in her most persuasive manner she added, "But I have another boy . . ."

"I don't want to hear about a boy," retorted Ethel. "I want George Peppard!"

"But Robert Redford would be so marvelous in this part!"

"We want a star!"

"I know, but Redford's so right. Can't he just read for you?"

Monique smiles as she remembers. "I drove them crazy until they finally agreed to let Redford read for the part. It was set up and I was more nervous than I'd ever been for a client. I was so sure he was right, but you never know what *they're* going to think." Finally, Redford walked in and Monique asked him how it went.

"It went fine," answered Redford. Then he added with resignation, "But they want a star."

The call from CBS came through while Redford was still in Monique's office, offering him the part and scale pay. "It was practically no money," says Monique. "But it was a golden opportunity for Redford."

To prepare for the part of the Nazi soldier, Redford followed a neighbor's German gardener for days to get his accent down pat. "I said in the show that I was from Bavaria," says Redford, "because that's where the gardener was from."

The effort paid off. When the show was aired on May 18, 1960, Redford's performance created a sensation and won him rave reviews—even though he was not the star of the production.

Jack Gould in the *New York Times* said, "As the young Nazi lieutenant with a conscience, Mr. Redford, a newcomer to the ranks of TV stars, made an exceptional contribution in his depiction of a man trying to reconcile a personal code with military brutality." The *Hollywood Reporter* noted, "It remained for newcomer Robert Redford, as a 'human' Nazi sergeant, to almost steal the show with his performance in this, his TV debut."

The extent of his success in the role is marked by the fact that shortly after, when Monique submitted his name for another role, the casting director expressed surprise. "But how can we use Redford in this part? He has a German accent!"

As he had been with Julie Harris, Redford was somewhat in awe of his co-star Charles Laughton. "I'd been awed by others too, like Greer Garson. But I think what finally cured me of that was when I slapped Charles Laughton. I was supposed to slap him on the show and during rehearsals I just went through the motions. When it came time to go on the air live, he wanted to know what I planned to do. I said, 'Well, I'll just give you a light slap,' and he said, 'No, I don't like to be hit. You'll have to work something out—I can't be touched, I hate it. I'm sorry, but it's your problem, you'll have to work it out.'"

Redford told the director and he almost fainted— they were minutes away from going on the air. When the moment came, on live TV, Redford looked at Laughton and Laughton looked at Redford and there was a look in Laughton's eyes—Well, what have you decided to do? As an actor, Redford had no choice—he

With Roberta Shore on *The Virginian*

slugged Laughton as hard as his character should have. "It shocked him and me and the people on the set," laughs Redford. "It was very effective for him dramatically, I must say. He didn't miss a beat—he played to the moment beautifully.

"When it was over I went to apologize and he stopped me and said, 'Don't apologize—you did what you had to do.' And that was the end of it. He was very nice. Anyway, after that I stopped being in awe of people."

Redford had no trouble getting roles after the raves of *Enemies*. But he was becoming concerned about typecasting. "The agencies weren't interested in versatile actors, because they couldn't make any money with versatile actors. Music Corporation of America, the gigantic agency, put tags on everybody that came through, like cattle: this was the All-American Boy, this is the boy next door, and this is a freak so we'll give him all the freak parts. I was labeled the All-American Boy Next Door, but since I never cared much for those kinds of guys, I started to play killers to get away from that. But then suddenly I was just this neurotic guy and wasn't being sent any other scripts."

But the critics continued to notice Redford and single him out for praise, even when his role was relatively small. One part interested him, even though it was not far from the typecast image he was trying to avoid, because he felt he could do a little extra with it. On *The Breaking Point,* he played Roger, a sadist who preys on the other patients in group therapy. "If it had been a straight sadist, I wouldn't have been interested," says Redford. "Roger is not out–and–out disturbed from beginning to end. He's intriguing because he attacks psychiatry, is a highly intelligent individual and would have a lot to offer if he wasn't blocked by his viciousness.

"Viewers see a lot of mean guys on TV, so I tried to play Roger for charm and ability, too, to make the role interesting and help the audience to understand Roger's mechanism a little better."

A complaint Redford made to Hesseltine during his television days was that he was receiving very little direction and felt adrift. "Nobody knows how to direct you because everything you do is so right," Hesseltine told him.

"It seemed I was either being over–directed or under-directed at this point. Someone who did nothing with me made me nervous. I thought, Well, why aren't they directing me? I should be getting direction because I'm new. If I got too much I hated it and if I got too little I'd get paranoid. It was very contradictory."

Whatever the extent of his direction, several of Redford's TV efforts are memorable. One of these is *The Voice of Charlie Pont,* an Alcoa Premiere presentation on October 25, 1962 co-starring Bradford Dillman and Diana Hyland. Redford won an Emmy

nomination as Best Supporting Actor for the drama.

Although Redford's television career can, on the whole, be characterized as successful, there was one aspect of it that was not. In early 1960, a desperately broke Redford went to Jean Thomas, a well-known commercial agent, and presented himself to her in the hope of gaining some work in the lucrative TV commercial market. Thomas thought he'd be fine for "Mr. and Mrs. America bits," as she puts it, and began sending him around to casting agents.

Their response was underwhelming. "He's good-looking," they'd say, "but there's nothing really special about him. I've got a dozen guys here just as good as he is." Thomas sent Redford out twenty-five or thirty times, and always with the same reaction. "It got so I was embarrassed to call him," she says. "Finally, I gave up. I knew Redford was special, but advertising guys are idiots. They're the last people who can appreciate a new talent."

Today, Ms. Thomas says, advertising people call her and ask for "a Robert Redford type." This never fails to make her furious and she yells back at them, "You asshole! When I had *Redford* you didn't want him. If I had a new Redford now you wouldn't appreciate him. And I certainly wouldn't waste anybody that good on *commercials!*"

Since 1964, Redford has concentrated on his movie career. He feels he got a good deal out of his TV experiences. "It was a training ground. You had to realize that at best you could only give about fifty percent of yourself because of the time factor, the limitations, the speed. So my attitude was that I used it as a training ground to make me learn to work quickly and deliver the maximum in a short amount of time, achieve full characterizations with very little to work with and very little time in which to do it. I guess I'd say that I learned a lot of my craft for film in television.

"I was fortunate enough to get into television at the very end of live, because there was a stimulation to going live on camera. It was very edgy and challenging and good."

Once live TV began to be phased out, Redford no longer found TV interesting. He turned down an offer of $150,000 for five years to star in *The Virginian.* "The money is nice," Redford was quoted at the time, "but I don't want to be out of the theater for five years. I want to build slowly and become a dramatic star."

He decided to go back to Broadway to do *Barefoot in the Park.* His agents thought he was crazy. "They said to me, 'What do you want to go back to Broadway for when you're carving out a career in TV? You can go on to the movies from TV if you stick with it.' But I wanted to go back to the stage. And it was the success of *Barefoot in the Park* that helped me break into the movies. It all happened pretty much the way I wanted it to."

THE DEPUTY

"The Last Gunfight"
April 30, 1960 (NBC)

An ex-gunfighter is challenged to a duel by a brash young gunman on the make.

Simon Fry, Henry Fonda; *Clay McCord,* Allen Case; *Johnny Dean,* Charles McGraw; *David Crawford,* Paul Clark; *Bill Johnson,* Robert Redford; *Helen Ivers,* Monica Lewis; *Haskins,* Perry Ivins.

HALLMARK HALL OF FAME

"Captain Brassbound's Conversion."
May 2, 1960 (NBC)

The mention of Captain Brassbound's name instills terror in the hearts of men everywhere — it is rumored that he is a pirate, and a fearsome one at that. Lady Cicely Waynflete, however, doesn't think twice when the Captain and his men are assigned to escort her across Morocco: she's never heard of him, and believes that all men are basically good. Their meeting creates conflict of a kind Capt. Brassbound never experienced. George Bernard Shaw's comedy was adapted by Theodore Apstein. This final "Hallmark Hall of Fame" episode was produced by George Schaefer and ran 90 minutes.

Lady Cicely Waynflete, Greer Garson; *Captain Brassbound,* Christopher Plummer; *Capt. Hamlin Kearney,* Loring Smith; *Sir Howard Hallam,* Felix Aylmer; *Rankin,* Liam Redmond; *Drinkwater,* George Rose; *Sheik Sidi El Assif,* Henry Brandon; *Cadi of Kintafi,* Howard Caine; *Marzo,* Robert Carricart; *Consul,* Harry Ellerbe; *Redbrook,* Chris Gampel; *Osman,* Patrick Westwood; *Johnson,* Douglas Henderson; *Officer,* William Lanteau; *Sailor,* Robert Redford.

PLAYHOUSE 90

"In the Presence of Mine Enemies"
May 18, 1960 (CBS)

It is the Second World War. The Warsaw ghetto in Nazi-occupied Poland. 500,000 people are imprisoned in a hundred-city-block area surrounded by a wall of concrete eight feet high. Every day more people are taken away to be experimented on, tortured and murdered. Amid this horror, the gentle head of an Orthodox Jewish congregation, Rabbi Adam Heller, attempts to keep his people as one and pass on to them his own hope, resolve, courage and belief in God. Directed by Fiedler Cook from a screenplay by Rod Serling.

Rabbi Adam Heller, Charles Laughton; *Paul Heller,* Arthur Kennedy; *Rachel Heller,* Susan Kohner; *Josef Chinik,* Oscar Homolka; *Captain Richter,* George Macready; *Emmanuel,* Sam Jaffe; *Sgt. Lott,* Robert Redford.

TATE

"The Bounty Hunter"
June 22, 1960 (NBC)

Believing that Tate has committed a crime and is on the run from law enforcement officials, Tom Sandee sets his mind on capturing him and bringing him to justice.

Tate, David McLean; *Tom,* Robert Culp; *Roberta McConnell,* Louise Fletcher; *Sean McConnell,* Robert Warwick; *John Torsett,* Robert Redford.

With Nancy McCarthy in "The Golden Deed"

MOMENT OF FEAR

"The Golden Deed"
July 1, 1960 (**NBC**)

A rich couple's child is rescued from drowning by a handsome stranger. Grateful, the couple take the man into their home and treat him as one of the family. Soon, however, they realize that he has involved them in a criminal act. Starring Macdonald Carey, Nancy McCarthy, Robert Redford.

(Facing Page) Another scene from "The Golden Deed"

With Raymond Burr and Thomas Henry in "Treacherous Toupee"

TATE

"Comanche Scalps"
August 19, 1960 (NBC)

Lucy was supposed to marry Amos Dundee. But when the wedding ceremony took place, the bridegroom was another Dundee — Amos' brother Tad. Amos didn't like that one bit — and now he plans to eliminate his brother.

Tate, David McLean; *Amos*, Frank Overton; *Tad*, Robert Redford; *Lucy*, Ann Whitfield; *William Easey*, Lane Bradford; *Comanche*, Leonard Nimoy.

PERRY MASON

"The Case of the Treacherous Toupee"
September 17, 1960 (CBS).

After two years, missing person Harley Basset shows up to return to his position of company president. No one is happy about it — not his wife, Sybil, who is involved with another, nor Peter Dawson, who has taken over the company presidency, nor his nephew Dick Hart, who has just married a social butterfly.

Mason, Raymond Burr; *Della*, Barbara Hale; *Drake*, William Hopper; *Tragg*, Ray Collins; *Harley*, Thomas B. Henry; *Sybil*, Peggy Converse; *Peter Dawson*,

With Raymond Burr and Cindy Robbins

Philip Ober; *Arthur Colemar*, Nelson Olmsted; *Dick Hart*, Robert Redford; *Ken Woodman*, Bert Freed; *Wilber Fenwick*, Lindsay Workman; *Stanley Roderick*, Jonathan Hole; *Teddi Hart*, Cindy Robbins; *Lorna Grant*, Dee Arlen.

"The Iceman Cometh."
Nov. 14 & 21, 1960. (NN)

A hot 1912 summer day. At Harry Hope's waterfront bar, derelicts sleep off the previous night's drunk in sleazy rooms above the saloon. When they awake, they battle their hangovers and talk hazily about the better life that is just around the corner for them. Today these men have particular reason to be cheerful — good ol' Hickey, a hardware drummer with money to spend and a cheerful, talkative disposition, is coming to town. Hickey always makes everybody feel better — whether through sheer optimism or a round of free drinks. But when Hickey arrives, things seem different. Hickey has changed, and his visit has unexpected ramifications for everyone at Harry Hope's. Directed by Sidney Lumet. Introduced by drama critic Brooks Atkinson.

Hickey, Jason Robards Jr.; *Larry Slade*, Myron McCormick; *Harry Hope*, Farrell Pelly; *Willie Oban*, James Broderick; *Piet Wetjoen (The General)*, Roland Winters; *Cecil Lewis (The Captain)*, Ronald Radd; *Jimmy Tomorrow*, Harrison Dowd; *Rocky Pioggi*, Tom Pedi; *Don Parritt*, Robert Redford; *Chuck Morello*, Michael Strong; *Pat McGloin*, Charles White; *Joe Mott*, Maxwell Glanville; *Hugo Kalmar*, Sorrell Booke; *Ed Mosher*, Walter Klavun; *Pearl*, Julie Bovasso; *Margie*, Hilda Brawner; *Cora*, Joan Copeland.

OUR AMERICAN HERITAGE

"Born A Giant"
December 2, 1960 (NBC)

The story of Andrew Jackson's life prior to his election as President of the United States. His life was freewheeling and adventurous, opening up the West and challenging a man who had insulted his wife to a duel to the death. Written by Mann Rubin.

Andrew Jackson, Bill Travers; *Rachel*, Barbara Rush; *Dickinson*, Farley Granger; *Overton*, Walter Matthau; *Captain Fort*, Robert Redford.

As Captain Fort on "Born A Giant," a segment of *Our American Heritage*

"Black Monday"
Jan. 16, 1961 (NN)

A typical school morning dawns bright in Bethlehem, a Deep South town steeped in tradition. But things will change as a Black child attempts to enter an all-white school against strong opposition. Originally intended for Broadway, the play is by Reginald Rose. David Susskind purchased the TV rights after an "Open End" discussion on school integration in New Orleans. Directed by Ralph Nelson. Running time: 2 hours. Produced on tape.

Arthur McGill: Pat Hingle; *Betty McGill*, Nancy Coleman; *Russell N. Porter*, Marc Connelly; *Alex-*

ander Dennison, Myron McCormick; *James*, Juano Hernandez; *George Dennison*, Robert Redford; *Jane Walker*, Ruby Dee; *Margaret Beane*, Frances Fuller; *Terry*, Joey Trent; *Policeman*, Edward Asner; *William May*, Arthur Tell; *William May Jr.*, Roy Johnson; *Jody*, Luke Halpin; *Bud*, James Kahn; *Virgil*, Andrew Prine; *Dr. Plummer*, House Jameson.

NAKED CITY

"Tombstone for a Derelict"
April 5, 1961 (ABC)

In the early morning hours, four young toughs come upon a vagrant. They offer him a cigarette, then each stabs him with a knife. Before leaving, they purposely leave behind a clue to their identities.

Flint, Paul Burke; *Parker*, Horace McMahon; *Arcara*, Harry Bellaver; *Baldwin*, Robert Redford; *Mrs. Larne*, Polly Rowles; *Josh*, Dan Jenkins; *Fred*, Bill Hinnant; *Charlie*, Don Gantry; *Lorne*, Bob Allen; *Streetcleaner*, Don Morgan.

THE AMERICANS

"The Coward"
May 8, 1961 (NBC)

George Harrod receives a last-minute reprieve just as he is about to be executed by a firing squad for cowardice in battle. No one knows why, but Harrod's sentence of death has been revoked.

Jeff, Dick Davalos; *Rowe*, Jackie Coogan; *George Harrod*, Robert Redford; *Captain Garber*, Carroll O'Connor; *Yonts*, L. Q. Jones; *Colonel*, Richard Hale.

WHISPERING SMITH

"The Grudge"
May 15, 1961 (NBC)

Smith learns that Ma Gates, widow of a man he brought to justice years before, is still seeking revenge and has come to town to avenge her husband.

Smith, Audie Murphy; *Richards*, Sam Buffington; *Johnny Gates*, Robert Redford; *Ma Gates*, June Walker; *Cora*, Gloria Talbott.

ROUTE 66

"First Class Mouliak"
October 20, 1961 (CBS)

Tod and Buzz go to work in a Pittsburgh steel mill for furnace men Jack and Mike. Soon, Mike's daughter is found dead and all evidence points to Jack's son Janosh as the killer.

Tod, Martin Milner; *Buzz*, George Maharis; *Jack*, Nehemiah Persoff; *Mike*, Martin Balsam; *Janosh*, Robert Redford; *Teresa*, Ann Dee.

BUS STOP

"The Covering Darkness"
October 22, 1961 (ABC)

Appearances can be deceiving. New arrivals Millie and Art Ellison seem like a lovely couple interested only in their baby. In reality, however, they are a nasty twosome mainly interested in the money some people in the town recently won in a sweepstakes.

Grace, Marilyn Maxwell; *Mayberry*, Rhodes Reason; *Wagner*, Richard Anderson; *Elma*, Joan Freeman; *Millie*, Barbara Baxley; *Art*, Robert Redford; *Ma Cramer*, June Walker; *Esther*, Mary Gregory; *Mr. Bartel*, Paul Kent; *Mrs. Bartel*, Charlene Brooks; *Ed Miller*, Chris Bowler; *Jeff*, Bill Tyler.

ALFRED HITCHCOCK

"The Right Kind of Medicine"
December 19, 1961 (CBS)

Charlie Pugh breaks into a house and is surprised by the police. He shoots it out with them and manages to get away. Everything is fine except that he has been wounded, and he's going to have to have a doctor look at it real soon.

Charlie Pugh, Robert Redford; *Vernon*, Joby Baker; *Mr. Fletcher*, Russell Collins; *Dr. Vogel*, Gage Clark; *Witness*, Bernard Kates; *Police Lt.*, King Calder; *Sgt.*, Robert Karnes; *Officer*, Bert Remsen.

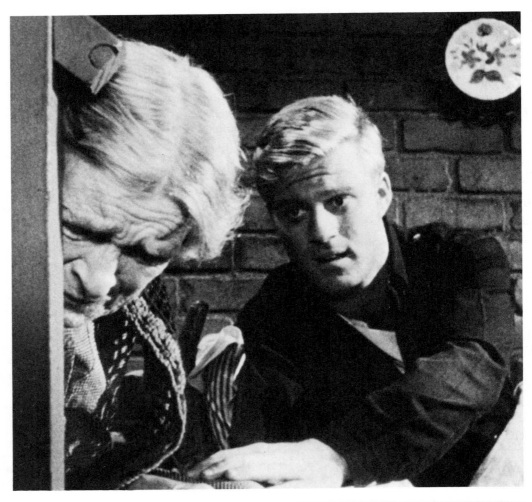

TWILIGHT ZONE

"Nothing In The Dark"
January 5, 1962 (CBS)

Wanda Dunn is reluctant to allow a wounded police-man into her tenement apartment. She does, however, and it seems to be the right decision. Until she discovers what his real intention is.

Wanda Dunn, Gladys Cooper; *Policeman,* Robert Redford.

The final scene of "Nothing in the Dark." Redford, not a policeman but Mr. Death in disguise, gently coaxes Gladys Cooper to join him

ALFRED HITCHCOCK

"A Piece of the Action"
September 20, 1962 (CBS)

Alice Marsden isn't at all happy with her husband Duke's gambling — and she sets out to do something about it.

Alice Marsden, Martha Hyer; *Duke Marsden,* Gig Young; *Chuck Marsden,* Robert Redford; *Ed Krutcher,* Gene Evans; *Nate,* Roger deKoven.

DR. KILDARE

"The Burning Sky"
October 4, 1962 (NBC)

Dr. Kildare decides that emergency surgery is necessary to save the life of Ellen Gates, victim of a fire at which Kildare's emergency medical team is working. But one of his assistants, Mark Hadley, refuses to assist in the operation.

Kildare, Richard Chamberlain; *Gillespie,* Raymond Massey; *Mark Hadley,* Robert Redford; *Roy Drummond,* Carroll O'Connor; *Jack Willis,* Steve Joyce; *Ellen Gates,* Harriet Day.

ALCOA PREMIER

"The Voice of Charlie Pont"
October 25, 1962 (ABC)

It seems that Harvard alumnus Charlie Pont has returned to Cambridge for a convivial visit with his friends Lisa and George Laurents. He is friendly and seemingly carefree. But his real purpose is to cause problems for an ex-girlfriend.

Charlie Pont, Bradford Dillman; *Lisa Laurents,* Diana Hyland; *George Laurents,* Robert Redford; *Brune,* Bill Bixby; *Sheila,* Cathie Merchant.

THE UNTOUCHABLES

"Snowball"
January 15, 1963 (ABC)

Jack Parker is still involved with the crowd at his former college. He is selling them illegal whiskey. Parker wants to involve Frank Nitti in a plan he has formulated to improve the alcohol trade on campus. Narrated by Walter Winchell.

Ness, Robert Stack; *Hobson,* Paul Picerni; *Rossi,* Nicholas Georgiade; *Youngfellow,* Abel Fernandez; *Jack Parker,* Robert Redford; *Frank Nitti,* Bruce Gordon; *Benny,* Gerald Hiken; *Capt. Johnson,* Robert Bice.

ALFRED HITCHCOCK

"A Tangled Web"
January 25, 1963 (CBS)

David Chesterman, playboy son of a wealthy socialite, runs off with the family maid, Marie. She is overjoyed — until she realizes that David is a criminal and on the run.

Karl Gault, Barry Morse; *David Chesterman,* Robert Redford; *Marie,* Zohra Lampert; *Ethel,* Gertrude Flynn.

DICK POWELL THEATER

"The Last of the Big Spenders"
April 16, 1963 (NBC)

Paul Oakland, a successful novelist, hasn't seen his son Nick in twenty years. After he learns that he has a bad heart condition and may die at any time, he makes efforts to get in touch with his son before it's too late.

Paul Oakland, Dana Andrews; *Adele Hughes,* Inger Stevens; *Nick Oakland,* Robert Redford; *Christopher Burton,* Herschel Bernardi; *Dr. Joseph Greer,* Norman Fell.

Five scenes from "A Tangled Web" on *Alfred Hitchcock* (With Zohra Lampert)

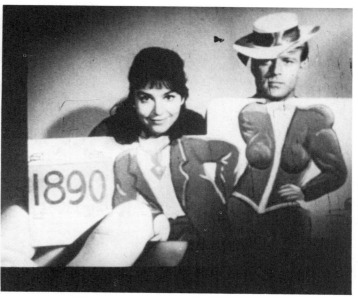

With Patricia Blair in "The Evil That Men Do," on *The Virginian*

BREAKING POINT

"Bird & Snake"
October 7, 1963 (ABC)

Roger Morton attends Doc Mac's group therapy sessions, ostensibly to come to grips with himself. But he actually has joined in order to vent his sadistic streak on the other members of the group.

Thompson, Paul Richards; *Raymer*, Eduard Franz; *Roger Morton*, Robert Redford; *Norma Rassiter*, Marisa Pavan; *Sam Keller*, Jack Weston; *Mrs. Levinson*, Connie Sawyer; *Judy Lawrence*, Mimi Dillard.

THE VIRGINIAN

"The Evil That Men Do"
October 16, 1963 (NBC)

Betsy finds herself attracted to Matthew Cordell, and the feelings are returned. But Cordell is a convict paroled in Judge Garth's custody, and serious problems arise.

Garth, Lee J. Cobb; *Betsy*, Roberta Shore; *Virginian*, James Drury; *Steve*, Gary Clarke; *Cordell*, Robert Redford; *Rita Marlow*, Patricia Blair.

NOTES

Other TV appearances by Robert Redford include a bit part on a segment of *Maverick* entitled "The Iron Hand," the pilot of the *Dr. Kildare* series, an *Armstrong Circle Theatre* entitled "Berlin—City With A Short Fuse," an episode of *Rescue 8* entitled "Breakdown" and a *Defenders* drama aired December 3, 1964 entitled "The Siege."

As Pvt. Roy Loomis

With Gavin MacLeod

With an unidentified extra

WAR HUNT

A United Artists Release of a T-D Enterprise Production (1962). 81 minutes.

CAST

Pvt. Raymond Endore, John Saxon; *Pvt. Roy Loomis,* Robert Redford; *Capt. Wallace Pratt,* Charles Aidman; *Sgt. Van Horn,* Sydney Pollack; *Pvt. Crotty,* Gavin MacLeod; *Charlie,* Tommy Matsuda; *Corp. Showalter,* Tom Skerritt; *Pvt. Fresno,* Tony Ray.

CREDITS

Produced by Terry Sanders; *Directed by* Denis Sanders; *Screenplay by* Stanford Whitmore; *Assistant Director:* Jack Bohier; *Photography* by Ted McCord; *Art Direction by* Edgar Lansbury; *Editing* by John Hoffman; *Sound:* Roy Meadows.

SYNOPSIS

Pvt. Roy Loomis joins a squad at the Korean front and is baffled by Raymond Endore. Endore is an unnaturally sullen soldier who goes on voluntary, solitary night patrols. His face blackened, he is at home in the night, silently killing enemies with a stiletto. Afterwards he remains by their bodies in mystical meditation. The military information he ultimately returns with has won him the high regard of Captain Pratt, whose attitude toward Endore is one of paternal indulgence. Although aware that the other men in the squad adhere to a "lay off Endore" policy in fear of this hero-killer paradox, and regardless of the danger both to the men and to Endore's own emotional stability, Pratt refuses to send him to a rest-and-rehabilitation station.

Endore has "adopted" an eight-year-old war orphan called Charlie whose parents were killed before his eyes. He guards the boy from the others with animal jealousy and when Loomis tries to befriend Charlie, Endore threatens his life.

The cease-fire order upsets Endore, who likes what he is doing. Violating the truce, he goes on patrol again that night, taking Charlie with him. Loomis knows he does not intend to come back. Fearful that the peace will be jeopardized, Pratt, Loomis and Sergeant Van Horn search no man's land. When they find the two, Endore seems finally to have slipped over the edge of reason. He refuses to obey Pratt's order to return and the captain tries to talk him down from the hill where he is making his stand. However, Pratt's "psychology" no longer works, and Endore pulls his stiletto. In the struggle that follows Pratt kills Endore. Charlie, seeing his "father" again taken from him, runs away. We last see him as a bitter, confused and agonized eight-year-old boy in no man's land.

By early 1961, Redford's television performances had earned him a reputation as a talented, hot new actor. It wasn't long before he had an offer to make his movie debut.

When he read the script of *War Hunt*, Redford was disappointed. "I'd just played a psycho on TV in *Black Monday*, and I thought that the killer was my part and that I was getting typecast again. But when I got to the studio, I discovered, to my joy, that John Saxon would do that part, and that I would be his observer, with all that happens reflected through my eyes."

Redford found the secondary role bland and undistinguished, and that became a challenge to him. Saxon, on the other hand, doesn't think the roles were that much different. "I was the protagonist and he was the antagonist. Or vice versa, depending on how you look at it."

Making a Hollywood movie didn't hold any

On location in California's Topanga Canyon: "It wasn't what I imagined a Hollywood movie to be like," says Redford

glamorous illusions for Bob. "I grew up around Hollywood and it was never the end of the rainbow for me—I knew there was no real rainbow. No one ever looked the way they did on screen."

Not that the filming of *War Hunt* was all that glamorous. A low budget effort, there was little money for any of the usual Hollywood embellishments. As Redford puts it, "It didn't seem like a movie. It wasn't at all what I imagined movies would be like. It was shot in three weeks for $250,000. We drove the actual army trucks. People took turns driving and making lunches. Francis Ford Coppola drove a truck. Noel Black held a reflector—he kept dropping it, actually. John Housman was hanging around, not doing anything. It was like a bunch of film students together. It really was a good feeling—but it wasn't a feeling of Hollywood."

In many ways, Redford didn't fit in too well with the rest of the cast. He was unfamiliar with the ways of moviemaking, and he was the most un-Hollywood of individuals. Quickly, he became friendly with another actor in the cast who was in the same boat, Sydney Pollack. It was the start of a long professional relationship.

With Sydney Pollack

With John Saxon

With Tommy Matsuda

Redford and Pollack stuck together in their befuddlement as well. "We were trained on Broadway," says Pollack, "where you sat down and discussed the parts and then rehearsed for four weeks. Now we were on a movie set where someone stands you someplace and you quick go through a scene, they shoot it and then they reshoot it again and again. It was such a different way of working, neither one of us knew what was going on.

"Neither Bob nor I thought much of the movie while we were making it. We couldn't see how all this was going to come out as a good film. But when we saw the finished product, I remember we both thought it was good."

Redford never did see the film in a theater. "I didn't dare go," he says. "I was afraid of overhearing some killing comment from the audience—the kind of crack I used to make as a kid."

Several months before the release of *War Hunt*, Lola gave birth to the Redfords' second child, a boy they named David James and nicknamed Jamie.

War Hunt was very well-received by the critics, several calling it a minor masterpiece. Redford's notices, as well, were glowing, and the film should have propelled him immediately into significant roles in major movies. There was, however, a complication.

Upon signing to do *War Hunt*, Redford entered into a contract with the Sanders brothers which called for him to do three more pictures for them. Redford, however, quickly balked. Pollack remembers that "The contract really gave Redford a pittance and he became hot pretty quickly after that. And the material they wanted him to do he didn't want to do."

Redford walked out on the contract, returning East to do *Sunday in New York* on Broadway. The Sanders brothers sued, and the lawsuits and counter-lawsuits went on for years before being settled. The litigation prevented Redford from making another movie until 1964.

REVIEWS

"If you want to see one of the most original and haunting war movies in years, don't miss *War Hunt*, which quietly bowed yesterday at the Trans-Lux Normandie. A singularly penetrating study of an American squad in action just before the cease-fire on the Korean Front, this modest United Artists release. . . must have been shot in a cornfield to the tune of a dime. And most of this little picture is pure, unvarnished gold. There is, in fact, a simple, blunt purity of structure and visuality seldom encountered on the screen.

"Mr. Saxon is aptly awesome in his meatiest screen role to date, and Mr. Redford, a movie newcomer, is excellent as his impressionable tormentor."
                                    HOWARD THOMPSON,
                                    The New York Times

"The youthful team of Denis Sanders, 33, the director, and his brother Terry, 29, the producer, has come up with an arresting war drama . . . rich in dramatic intensity. They have focused not so much on the physical scars of war—there is just one major battle scene—as on its traumatic effects on both the warrior and non-warrior.

"John Saxon, up to now little more than a teen-age idol, is first-rate in the difficult role of the psychopathic Endore. Robert Redford makes a noteworthy screen debut as Loomis . . ."
                                    ROBERT SALMAGGI,
                                    New York Herald Tribune

". . . a happy instance of stunning achievement on the part of two young filmmakers is evident in *War Hunt*, a tightly-packed, tensely drawn war drama . . . in which there is not one conspicuously conventional GI type. It reaches a rare emotional level—a kind of poetry—for this type of film."
                                    BOSLEY CROWTHER,
                                    The New York Times

"*War Hunt* . . . is a subtle, poignant, carefully engraved film that avoids both the fashionable giant-pore 'realism' of the French and Italians and the two day stubble 'realism' beloved by Hollywood. The background details are often masterly. There is a short, terrifying hand-to-hand fight between Loomis and a Chinese soldier. The nights are nights and the dawns are dawns. The camera is as matter-of-fact about wild flowers as it is about a dead man's face. . . Robert Redford, as Loomis, is appropriately all thumbs, good looks and milkfed intentions."
                                    The New Yorker

"Robert Redford has a translucent quality as the idealistic young soldier, whose few resources are nearly shattered by his exposure to the barbaric. A fine performance."
                                    Hollywood Reporter

SITUATION HOPELESS--
BUT NOT SERIOUS

A Paramount Release (1965) . 97 minutes.

CAST

Herr Frick, Alec Guinness; *Lucky,* Michael Connors; *Hank,* Robert Redford; *Edeltraud,* Anita Hoefer; *Lissie,* Mady Rahl; *Herr Neusel,* Paul Dahlke; *QM Master Sergeant,* Frank Wolff; *Sergeant,* John Briley; *Wanda,* Elisabeth Von Molo; *Senta,* Carola Regnier.

CREDITS

Produced and Directed by Gottfried Reinhardt; *Screenplay by* Silvia Reinhardt; *Adaptation by* Jan Lustig; *Based on the Novel* "The Hiding Place" by Robert Shaw; *Photography by* Kurt Hasse; *Costumes by* Ilse Dubois; *Assistant Producer:* Jose de Villaverde; *Assistant Director:* Henry Sokal; *Music by* Harold Byrns; *Editing by* Walter Boos; *Art Direction by* Rolf Zehetbauer.

SYNOPSIS

In November, 1944 the peaceful village of Altheim is the victim of an American airstrike, although the town contains only a sauerkraut factory.

One of the planes is shot down and two fliers—Lucky and Hank—elude German pursuers and hide out in the cellar of Herr Frick, a quiet, eccentric and unassuming shop-clerk still very much under the influence of his late mother's memory. After their pursuers are gone, Frick shuts his cellar door and "captures" the two Americans. This offers Frick a feeling of power; but more, the presence of two people for whom he can concern himself.

The war continues and Frick explains that to release them would only mean their capture by German officials. He provides food and lodging for his captives and they are momentarily satisfied.

Weeks and months pass. The war is over and Altheim is occupied by the American military government. Frick, now enjoying his mastery and the presence of Lucky and Hank, keeps up the illusion that the war is on. He hides his secret from his boss, Herr Neusel, and his fellow employee Edeltraud. He makes up stories of German conquests to justify keeping his captives in the cellar.

On Christmas, six years later, Frick is on the hunt for a Christmas goose for Hank and a girl for Lucky as an equally suitable holiday accommodation. He gets the goose, and after explaining that he isn't the prospective lover, that the real lover is chained to another man, and that the "accommodation" must not speak a word, Frick is thrown out of the Daffy-Dil Club by Lissie, the bordello madame.

Frick then has a heart attack and lies in a hospital unconscious for days while his wards starve. He comes to, rushes out of the hospital, steals a bike and rides home. Two policemen follow. Frick, realizing that the jig is up, releases his two "friends," provides them with warm clothing, and sends them on their way—without telling them the truth about the war.

When Hank and Lucky see Germany now rebuilding, streets loaded with new cars, packed store windows, they are convinced Frick has told them the truth: Germany has won the war. They get to a lake, think it's Lake Constance on the German-Swiss border; they evade Wanda, an impossible existentialist teenager, and Senta, her bratty kid sister, and get across the lake only to be accosted by an army of SS troops —involved in an American movie production about World War II. They fight their way through several hundred "troops"—in reality bit players—and finally get to "freedom."

After catching up with years of history, Hank and Lucky throw a belated victory party. The only man who can really tell the story, the butler, enters. It is Herr Frick, now employed by Hank. The three men are united in friendship.

Michael Connors as Lucky and Redford as Hank—unlucky WW II flyers

74

Shauna, Lola, Jamie and Mrs. Michael Connors visit the stars on location in Munich

75

After leaving *Barefoot in the Park*, Redford traveled to Germany to film *Situation Hopeless—But Not Serious*, a comedy based on Robert Shaw's best-selling novel *The Hiding Place*. The film was the project of noted German director Gottfried Reinhardt, who served as director and producer and whose wife Silvia wrote the screenplay. Redford received third billing behind Academy Award winning actor Alec Guinness as Herr Frick and Michael Connors as Redford's co-flier.

Redford enjoyed the location filming in Munich and various picturesque German hamlets. "I always like going on location—you get a chance to learn. I picked up the language pretty well, learned a lot about culture and met some interesting people." He stayed in the same apartment he had while he was in Germany as an art student six years earlier. "My stay in Europe had been difficult, but it was a good time, one of the happiest times of my life. Being unhappy at the time was just part of the growing process. Going back there just allowed me to sort of do things with a little more comfort, not with my back against the wall and the wolf at the door and all that. I had more freedom to try things like certain restaurants and higher parts of the culture. It was a nice chance to continue what I'd started before. The actual film experience, though, was the least of the virtues."

Redford found working with Gottfried Reinhardt unsatisfying. "He was heavy-handed and had a rather Teutonic sense of comedy timing which may have been right for some things but it wasn't the kind of humor I felt was applicable to that film. And what he was doing with the camera seemed static, conventional." To relieve his boredom during filming Redford spent lulls sketching Guinness and Connors, and his drawings were used in the film as the work of his character Hank, who drew to fill his time as a prisoner.

Mike Connors and Redford got along well. "I like him a lot," says Redford. "He's a really nice guy." And there was a great deal of mutual respect between Alec Guinness and Redford. The veteran and the relative newcomer discussed acting, first nights, reviewers and theories of comedy in a conversation published in *Show*'s December 1964 issue. Guinness warned Redford, "I'm afraid you'll find that film comedy can be particularly difficult and frustrating—one's performance is fragmented up into so many little twenty- and thirty-second bits and pieces. It's immensely difficult to sustain a properly balanced comic character throughout the three months or so it takes to make a film. In fact, doing a film comedy can be rather an ordeal."

As it turned out, the only ordeal concerning *Situation Hopeless* was sitting through it. The film's comic premise became strained and the talents of the principals could go only so far toward saving an embarrassing script. The film was shown to reviewers and was panned. As a result, it was not released to the public. "I didn't feel badly about that at all," says Redford. "I guess I felt as we were doing it that it might not be releasable. But I didn't trust my feelings because it was just my second film."

Four years later, to cash in on Redford's *Butch Cassidy* popularity, Paramount decided to release the film on a double bill with *Oh Dad, Poor Dad, Mama's Hung You In The Closet and I'm Feeling So Sad*. A Paramount spokesman explained, rather lamely, that "Somehow the film was held up every time it was due to be brought to the public." Redford found Paramount's action "fairly typical. It's all part of the 'cash in' syndrome around here."

The film wasn't available for review screenings the second time around, and it failed to attract any attention. Some news was made when Robert Shaw requested that his name be removed from the advertising campaign.

REVIEWS

"If *The Collector* had been done as a Doris Day-Rock Hudson comedy, it would have wound up as a first cousin to *Situation Hopeless—But Not Serious*, a film that merits our attention only because Sir Alec Guinness is ensnared therein. The airmen—Robert Redford as an intellectual multi-millionaire captain and Michael Connors as a lowbrow greasemonkey sergeant—are dull clichés and, with the exception of Mady Rahl as the prostitute, the other characters, whether as Germans or American occupation troops, are heavy-handed caricatures. The movie was made entirely on location in Germany. Like the situation, it is hopeless."

JUDITH CRIST,
New York Herald Tribune

"Robert Shaw, the versatile and talented British actor-writer, now has the somewhat dubious satisfaction of knowing that his highly praised first novel, *The Hiding Place,* has been both televised (1960) and filmed. The TV version disappointed this newspaper's appraiser and the movie version . . . is a mild, pat comedy that is rarely as funny or satirical as its title."

A. H. WEILER,
The New York Times

(Right) Lost in an
unfriendly village

Trying to escape
from Herr Frick's
bondage

"*Situation Hopeless—But Not Serious*, at RKO theatres, could more aptly be titled *Situation Hopeless—and Not Funny*. Producer-Director Gottfried Reinhardt thinks he has made a comedy-satire . . . he has labored mightily over it. But from the opening credits as the fliers float earthward, the whole film falls with a thud.

"It isn't the fault of the actors. Alec Guinness plays the eccentric German brilliantly without over-clowning . . . Robert Redford and Michael Connors are easy to like as the affable fliers."

FRANCES HERRIDGE,
New York Post

Situation Hopeless—But Not Serious is neither very funny nor deadly serious, falling with a dismaying thud between the two and leaving you in the end with the feeling that somewhere, somehow, somebody just blew it . . . Michael Connors and Robert Redford (the latter recruited from *Barefoot in the Park*) just roar and rant at each other in the confines of their imprisonment, neither of them being very attractive."

LEO MISHKIN,
New York Morning Telegraph

Escaped at last

All is forgiven as Herr Frick serves as Lucky's butler

INSIDE DAISY CLOVER

A Warner Bros. Release of a Park Place Production (1966). In Technicolor and Panavision. 128 minutes.

CAST

Daisy, Natalie Wood; *Raymond Swan*, Christopher Plummer; *Wade Lewis*, Robert Redford; *Baines*, Roddy McDowall; *The Dealer*, Ruth Gordon; *Melora Swan*, Katharine Bard; *Gloria Goslett*, Betty Harford; *Dancer*, Paul Hartman; *Harry Goslett*, John Hale; *Cop*, Harold Gould; *Old Lady in Hospital*, Ottola Nesmith; *Cynara*, Edna Holland; *Milton Hopwood*, Peter Helm.

CREDITS

Produced by Alan J. Pakula; *Directed by* Robert Mulligan; *Screenplay by* Gavin Lambert; *Based On His Novel*; *Photography by* Charles Lang; *Costumes by* William Thomas; *Miss Wood's Wardrobe by* Edith Head; *Music by* Andre Previn; *Songs by* Dory and Andre Previn; *Musical Numbers Staged by* Herbert Ross; *Assistant Director:* Joseph E. Kenny; *Edited by* Aaron Stell, A.C.E.

Daisy and Wade at their first meeting

SYNOPSIS

Daisy Clover, a fifteen-year-old rebel with a cause, has no one to celebrate her birthday with. She strolls down an amusement pier, singing to herself, and for a moment the singing makes the world less of a garbage dump to her. She stops at a recording booth and as a present to herself makes a disc by singing one of her favorite songs. As a lark, she sends the record to a Hollywood film company conducting a talent search.

Daisy returns to her trailer where she and her mother, The Dealer, live. Her strange and somewhat addled mother has forgotten Daisy's birthday. There is no celebration, so Daisy goes out to spend the evening with admirer Milton Hopwood, Jr.

The studio hears Daisy's record and invites her to a screen and song test. Studio aide Walter Baines brings Daisy to meet film mogul Raymond Swan and his wife, Melora. The test is excellent and Swan signs the unkempt youngster.

Daisy's sister, Gloria, and her husband, Harry, decide that The Dealer is the wrong sort of person to have around a rising young star. They arrange with Swan to have her committed to a sanitarium. Though Daisy is furious and heartbroken, she is unable to do anything about it. A few months later Daisy completes her first picture. Swan hosts a lavish party to introduce his new star to Hollywood. At his home Daisy meets screen idol Wade Lewis and runs off with him for the evening.

Song-and-dance roles zoom Daisy to stardom. She is expected to attend the premiere of her latest film and instead spends the night with Wade on his boat. The next morning she wakes up and finds him gone. Months pass and her career soars higher. She hears nothing from the traveling Wade. One day he returns; they reconcile and she again spends the night with him on his boat.

Under pressure from Swan, Wade proposes to Daisy. They are married at the Swan mansion and go to Arizona for their honeymoon. But Wade soon deserts her, leaving her sleeping in a motel in the desert.

Daisy returns to Hollywood and attempts to pull herself together, taking The Dealer out of the rest home to live with her. But one night Daisy comes home and finds her mother dead. Her world collapses.

She breaks down during a recording session at the studio. She takes refuge in her beach home, refusing to communicate with anyone. Swan threatens to end her career unless she finishes a film. Fed up with everything, Daisy attempts suicide by putting her head in an oven. Even this goes wrong for Daisy—she is interrupted by doorbell and telephone rings. She gives up and goes out of the house, leaving the gas on. Moments later, she hears a sound and turns in time to see the house blowing up.

It is April 10, 1938. Daisy's career is over. She is almost seventeen.

Visiting The Dealer in the rest home
(with Ruth Gordon, Ottola Nesmith
and Natalie Wood)

Inside Daisy Clover presented Redford with a dilemma. It was a chance to play opposite Hollywood's hottest female star, Natalie Wood, in a major production for a salary of $75,000. But all his advisers were against his playing the role because the character, movie star Wade Lewis, was a homosexual.

Redford, however, saw the part as a challenge—if he could play it his way. "Everyone was saying 'don't do it.' As a matter of fact, I didn't play the character as a homosexual. I'd been around Hollywood enough to know that there was this whole breed of people who were narcissists. Constantly on the take, never on the give. No one was prepared to go along with that interpretation of the role. But I said to Alan Pakula, the producer, 'Gavin Lambert wrote this guy as a homosexual. Now maybe he's got strong feelings, but if that's what you want to do with it, then I'm not interested. I'm interested in playing, if anything, someone who bats ten different ways: children, women, dogs, cats, men, anything that salves his ego. Total narcissism.' "

That is how Redford acted the role, but, after filming was completed, an additional scene was shot to explain that Wade Lewis was homosexual. Redford was very displeased. "Since I hadn't played it that way, it knocked hell out of the character, the interpretation.

"The filmmakers weakened in regard to the commitment they had made. They wanted something strong that wasn't in the film they'd made—something shocking, to juice it up. And I remember being quite upset about it because it was done without my knowledge and it was re-interpreting the role, which isn't fair. It isn't fair to an actor to direct him and agree on a concept and play it all the way through and have the film finished and then come around from behind without telling him and put something in that re-interprets the role.

"It was another of those little incidents that made me not very anxious to continue in movies. After the first three films I did in Hollywood I wasn't too enthused about continuing on as an actor. That's why I took off for a year."

During the filming, Mike Nichols visited Redford on the set. They discussed the possibility of Redford playing the role of Nick in *Who's Afraid of Virginia Woolf?*, which Nichols was set to direct. Redford declined because he didn't like the play or the character. Then Nichols told him that there was a great deal of industry talk in New York about Redford's "star quality" in *Inside Daisy Clover*. Nichols told Redford, "Everybody I run into tells me, 'Wait until you see Redford in *Daisy Clover*. He jumps right off the screen.' "

Redford told Nichols that was very interesting,

because at that point he hadn't been in a single foot of film.

During the filming, Redford and Natalie Wood became close friends, a friendship that lasts to this day. While filming a scene in which Wade and Daisy are out on a sailboat, a severe swell rose, separating them from the rest of the crew. Director Robert Mulligan remembers that panic ensued: "There was no way we could get them off the boat, and the lines to keep them in place were breaking right and left. One of the crew members broke his leg as a cable snapped and we had to rush him to a hospital. All the time we were worrying about Bob and Natalie, and it was obvious that she was terrified and he was having a great time. He was laughing like hell and turning the whole thing into a wonderful adventure. When he found out about the broken leg, of course, he didn't think it was so funny, but I think his sense of fun kept Natalie from having a heart attack."

During a day of shooting at a Santa Monica beach, Redford had a chance to relive part of his childhood. "Once when I was little," he says, "I met a boy dressed in a sailor suit standing in front of a carousel near the ocean. I asked him 'How old are you?' And he asked, 'How old are *you*?' We went round and round in a circle until finally I told him 'Four,' and then he said, 'I'm five. I'm older than you are!' and walked away. We went down there to shoot a scene, and there was that old carousel, closed down, rusty, faded. I went over to the man who was there and asked if he would start it up for me. 'You with the movie company?' he asked and I said 'Yes.' He said, 'Got a part?' and I said 'Yes.' He said, 'Okay, come on,' and he started it up. I got up on a wooden horse and rode around on the carousel for twenty minutes, thinking of the good old days."

Inside Daisy Clover opened to negative reviews and was not a success. Redford's notices, however, were excellent. Typical of comments was Pauline Kael's. She said, "Robert Redford, in one of the most cryptic roles ever written, gives the only fresh performance in *Inside Daisy Clover*."

Redford feels the film suffered from trying to be too many things at the same time. Was it a searing, tough, realistic look at Hollywood or a kind of fantasy, slightly camp? "Half the picture was doing one thing and half was doing another," says Redford, "and I think it confused itself and probably the audience."

At that point in his career, Redford didn't feel it his place to criticize. "I had instincts about the picture I wasn't voicing. I'd think, I question this, but I never raised it because I didn't feel qualified. I was just there as an actor and I was hired and that was it. I wasn't really sure what was wrong. I just thought, This is strange. Now, looking back, I can articulate

Bob and Natalie Wood relax on the set

On Wade's yacht

With Katharine Bard

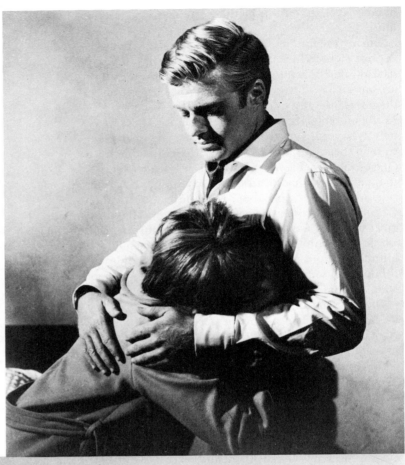

what it was I felt. But then I didn't know."

Redford received his first award for this film, the Hollywood Foreign Press Association's Golden Globe as "Star of the Future." He did not attend the televised ceremonies, but it didn't really matter: the award for his category was given five minutes after the show went off the air.

REVIEWS

"By the Hollywood standards of 1936—the time of the story—the picture would have been pretty bad, and by today's Hollywood standards it is still pretty bad, its weaknesses all the more embarrassing for being inadvertent . . . Natalie Wood isn't very plausible either as a fifteen-year-old or as a singer, and Mr. Plummer is as simperingly ineffectual here as he was in *The Sound of Music*. Others in the cast are Robert Redford, Roddy McDowall, Ruth Gordon and Katherine Bard. Poor things."

BRENDAN GILL,
The New Yorker

". . . it seems that in the years of its decline, Hollywood has come to take a perverse pride in its rottenness, as if it were the last thing in which it still truly leads the world . . . *Inside Daisy Clover* is . . . a not-bad idea gone wrong in compromised execution, but occasionally redeemed by graceful performances . . . the satirical gears keep slipping and, motor racing madly, the picture repeatedly stalls and becomes conventional, conventionalized drama of a rather dreary sort. There are redeeming moments in the performances of Christopher Plummer, Robert Redford and Katherine Bard. Together they cannot save a picture trying to be too many things at once, but they do make it intermittently enjoyable."

RICHARD SHICKEL,
Life

As movie star Wade Lewis, costumed for a new role

THE CHASE

(Above and right) As Bubber Reeves, escaped convict on the run

A Columbia Release of a Horizon Picture (1966). In Panavision and Technicolor. 135 minutes.

CAST

Calder, Marlon Brando; *Anna,* Jane Fonda; *Bubber,* Robert Redford; *Val Rogers,* E.G. Marshall; *Ruby Calder,* Angie Dickinson; *Emily Stewart,* Janice Rule; *Mrs. Reeves,* Miriam Hopkins; *Mary Fuller,* Martha Hyer; *Damon Fuller,* Richard Bradford; *Edwin Stewart,* Robert Duvall; *Jason "Jake" Rogers,* James Fox; *Elizabeth Rogers,* Diana Hyland; *Briggs,* Henry Hull; *Mrs. Briggs,* Jocelyn Brando; *Verna Dee,* Katherine Walsh; *Cutie,* Lori Martin; *Paul,* Marc Seaton; *Seymour,* Paul Williams; *Lem,* Clifton James; *Mr. Reeves,* Malcolm Atterbury; *Mrs. Henderson,* Nydia Westman; *Lester Johnson,* Joel Fluellen; *Archie,* Steve Ihnat; *Moore,* Maurice Manson; *Sol,* Bruce Cabot; *Slim,* Steve Whittaker; *Mrs. Sifftifieus,* Pamela Curran; *Sam,* Ken Renard.

CREDITS

Produced by Sam Spiegel; *Directed by* Arthur Penn; *Screenplay by* Lillian Hellman; *Based on the Novel and Play by* Horton Foote; *Photography by* Joseph La Shelle; *Assistant Director:* Russell Saunders; *Costumes by* Donfeld; *Art Direction by* Robert Luthardt; *Music by* John Barry; *Edited by* Gene Milford, A.C.E.

SYNOPSIS

When Bubber Reeves escapes from the state penitentiary after a murder committed by another escaping convict, his flight opens a Pandora's box of evil in the small, narrow-minded southwestern community where his wife Anna is having an affair with Jason Rogers. Rogers is the son of local cattle and oil baron Val Rogers. Sheriff Calder, refusing advice from the elder Rogers, takes on the town singlehandedly to save Bubber's life from gathering lynch mobs; but Calder is severely beaten.

Others affected by Bubber's suspected presence in the town include Emily, wanton wife of the weak Edwin Stewart. She is having an affair with Damon Fuller while his wife, Mary, is turning into an alcoholic. Bubber's mother believes that Calder will kill her son when he is recaptured. Elizabeth, Jason's wife, is trying to escape from her loveless marriage. Briggs, the town realtor, cynically watches as the lynch spirit grows. Calder's wife Ruby pleads with her husband to stop fighting the anti-Reeves fever in the town.

Soon, Bubber is trapped in the town's junkyard. Anna and Jason try to help him and Calder tries to protect him from the gathering mob, which consists not only of the town's "better" citizens but teenagers as well. An explosion kills Jason, ending Val Rogers' dreams for the future.

Calder brings Bubber in, but the convict is killed on the jailhouse steps by drunks. Defeated, but a victor in another sense, Calder leaves town with Ruby; he has, at last, preserved his own integrity.

With Marlon Brando

Few films have seemed more destined for success —both artistic and commercial—than *The Chase*. The talent involved included producer Sam Spiegel of *Bridge on the River Kwai* and *Lawrence of Arabia*, and director Arthur Penn. The screenplay was by Lillian Hellman (her first after a long period of blacklisting) and the stars were Marlon Brando, Jane Fonda, E.G. Marshall, Angie Dickinson, Janice Rule and Redford.

Originally, Redford was offered the role of Jake Rogers, but he turned it down in favor of the smaller part of Bubber Reeves. He felt Bubber was the more interesting character of the two. "The part had a kind of special meaning for me as well," he says. "I spent some time in jail, just overnight, when I used to get in trouble as a kid. I understood what made Bubber what he was. I felt close to him."

Redford's character, although the catalyst of all the action in *The Chase*, appears on film infrequently, and the part required his presence for just four weeks of the twenty-two week shooting schedule. The first two months, he worked seven days. "I had to keep introducing myself when I went on the set, but I was

With Jane Fonda during a break in filming

on salary all that time so I wasn't unhappy."

A good deal of the part called for Redford to be on the run through the outskirts of town. "I didn't see much of Arthur Penn," he says. "I was up in Chico, California, happily, I might add, running through rice fields alone with the second unit crew. The only things I talked to were animals for the most part. Arthur wasn't there. He was down in Hollywood shooting principal photography."

Once filming was completed, it became apparent that, despite the talents involved in the production, *The Chase* was not all it could have been. At its first screening, in fact, the film was greeted with outright hostility by the audience, with jeers drowning out the last few minutes. The reviews were vicious, with a few commending several of the actors, especially Redford. He was about the only participant to come out of *The Chase* unscathed.

"It did have a lot going for it on paper," says Redford, "but I was never that taken with the script. I thought it suffered from the 'kitchen sink syndrome'—it tried to do too much. I think it could have done well with a quarter of the relationships. Essentially the hub of that film was centered around four people—the character I played, his wife, the father on the hill and the sheriff. And it *was* a chase. But the movie wasn't a chase—it just tried to bring in all the liberal concepts of civil rights."

After the film's failure, Arthur Penn complained loudly that full control of the film had not been given him by Sam Spiegel. "I have never made a film under such unspeakable conditions," he said. "I was used merely to move the actors around like horses." Penn was excluded from the final editing of the film.

Redford blames Penn in part for the "unspeakable conditions": "He didn't have to work under them. He could have changed them—or left. I don't think retrospective criticism was very admirable in this case. If it was me, I would have said, 'Either let me direct this film my way, or I'm leaving.' "

REVIEWS

"Everything is intensely overheated in the new Marlon Brando film, *The Chase*, which blowtorched its way into the Sutton and the Victoria yesterday. The only thing that is not overheated—at least, I don't think it will be—is the audience's reaction. This is a picture to leave you cold. Yes, it's a phony, tasteless movie, and it is unbelievably played by E. G. Marshall as the town's Mr. Gotrocks, James Fox (the English actor) as his son, Jane Fonda as the trollop wife of the fugitive (who is frying her own kettle of fish with Mr. Fox) , Robert Redford as the homing fugitive and

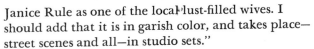

Janice Rule as one of the local lust-filled wives. I should add that it is in garish color, and takes place—street scenes and all—in studio sets."

BOSLEY CROWTHER,
The New York Times

"Penn has simply tried for realism, and he has poured it on. He has an uncommonly good cast of big names and small, headed by Brando in one of his very fine stints . . . Robert Redford is very good and defeated as Bubber."

ARCHER WINSTEN,
New York Post

"*The Chase* is contrivance from beginning to end—a successful contrivance, I am quick to report, a series of shameless cliches and stereotypes balled up with such skill that you roll right along with them to a smashing conclusion. And hate yourself for having been hooked a half hour later. The big-name performers offer professionalism too, some with their accustomed polish, some in a manner befitting the stereotypes they are called upon to be. A few performers manage a suggestion of depth in their roles. Robert Redford is, at very least, the most nearly sympathetic character on hand as the bad boy. We end *The Chase* tense, exhausted and frustrated, in sequence. Well, why look back? At worst, you've had a run for your money."

JUDITH CRIST,
New York Herald Tribune

"Robert Redford . . . gives the film's best perform-

ance and the best, to date, of his still short screen career. He has an instinct for economy of dialogue delivery and, alone on the screen during much of the earlier action and bypassed for lengthy sequences when the story deals with other plot elements, he so imprints his character on the viewer's mind that, upon re-entering the scene, his last-seen action is still clear to the memory. Even when he finally becomes involved with other cast members, his own performance dominates."

ROBE.,
Variety

"*The Chase* is no longer a modest failure. Thanks to the expenditure of a great deal of time, money and talent, it has been transferred into a disaster of awesome proportions . . . A valiant minority of the star cast—Miss Fonda, Robert Redford, James Fox, Angie Dickinson—try to keep their head while all about them are losing theirs. But their isolated moments of lucidity are no more effective against the fever than cold compresses; they relieve but cannot cure."

RICHARD SHICKEL,
Life

"*The Chase* is hardly more than *Peyton Place* with a Southern accent, an overblown, overstaged, over-acted, witless and preposterous hunk of drivel that utterly belies all the talents that went into its making . . . Robert Redford makes a handsome, if unconvincing, escaped convict."

LEO MISHKIN,
New York Morning Telegraph

On the final day of filming. Redford, Jane Fonda and James Fox cavort on the set

THIS PROPERTY IS CONDEMNED

A Paramount Pictures Release of a Seven Arts-Ray Stark Production (1966). In Technicolor. 110 minutes.

CAST

Alva Starr, Natalie Wood; *Owen Legate,* Robert Redford; *J. J. Nichols*, Charles Bronson; *Hazel Starr*, Kate Reid; *Willie Starr*, Mary Badham; *Knopke*, Alan Baxter; *Sidney*, Robert Blake; *Johnson*, John Harding; *Salesman*, Dabney Coleman; *Jimmy Bell*, Ray Hemphill; *Charlie Steinkamp*, Brett Pearson; *Tom*, Jon Provost; *Hank*, Quentin Sondergaard; *Max*, Michael Steen; *Lindsay Tate*, Bruce Watson.

CREDITS

Produced by John Houseman; *Directed by* Sydney Pollack; *Screenplay by* Francis Ford Coppola, Fred Coe, Edith Sommer; *Suggested by a one-act play* of Tennessee Williams; *Photography by* James Wong Howe, A.S.C.; *Music Scored by* Kenyon Hopkins; *Song "Wish Me A Rainbow"* by Jay Livingston and Ray Evans; *Costumes by* Edith Head; *Art Direction by* Hal Pereira, Stephen Grimes and Phil Jeffries; *Assistant Director*: Eddie Saeta; *Edited by* Adrienne Fazan.

SYNOPSIS

In the 1930s, thirteen-year-old Willie Starr is telling her friend Tom about the good times she and her family used to have at the boarding house they had nearby in Dodson, Miss. As she talks, we flashback to Owen Legate, a stranger, jumping off a freight train in the middle of Dobson.

Legate is there to lay off some railroad workers, but no one in the town is aware of this. He gets a room at the Starr boarding house and meets mother Hazel and Willie's older sister Alva, a charming flirt well aware of her reputation as the town's main attraction. Hazel is trying to get Alva hooked up with a middle-aged dud named Johnson who happens to have a lot of money, but Alva isn't interested.

Legate soon lets Alva know that he considers her a tart. Annoyed, she decides to give him a reason for his opinion and organizes a skinny-dipping party, at which she is propositioned by her mother's boyfriend J.J. Nichols. When Alva learns of Legate's mission, she confronts him with the information. But her attraction to him overrides her anger, and when he kisses her, she responds.

The next morning, the railroad men react angrily to their dismissal notices. Hazel is beside herself, since many of them are her boarders and this could mean the end of her place. She tries to get some money from Mr. Johnson. Meanwhile, Alva and Legate fall in love, and learn more about each other in an empty Pullman car. Alva confesses that more than anything else she wants to get away from Dodson.

Later, Hazel makes her deal with Johnson, and Legate is beaten up by five of the railroad men he fired. Alva, dressing his wounds, reiterates her desire to go to the big city. Owen decides he and Alva belong together.

Next morning Hazel finds Alva alone in Owen's room and they quarrel. Owen returns later with a ticket to New Orleans for Alva, but Hazel tells him Alva has changed her mind and is going to Memphis with Mr. Johnson. Without giving Alva a chance to explain, Owen leaves.

Crushed, Alva becomes the pawn in a cruel game of deceit, and desperately she marries J.J. Nichols. But she runs away from that rash marriage within a day to find her true love, Owen, in New Orleans. They are happy together until Hazel comes and tells Owen about Alva's secret marriage. Alva is wounded this time beyond endurance and runs away from Owen, who tries to prevent her from leaving.

Alva goes back to Dodson, disillusioned and used up by life, a cheap pickup. But she remains the pinnacle of glamor and enchantment to her worshipful sister Willie.

Redford as Owen Legate, Natalie Wood as Alva Starr

Natalie Wood's association with Bob on *Inside Daisy Clover* had been such a pleasant one that when she was asked to do an adaptation of Tennessee Williams' short play *This Property Is Condemned*, she insisted on Redford as her leading man. A long-time associate of Bob's says, "Women love to work with him because he doesn't come on to them. He just comes to work and is very considerate of everyone. Natalie really loved him. There weren't those ego entanglements there usually are when two stars are together on a set."

The film had a difficult time getting off the ground. It had originally been planned as a vehicle for Elizabeth Taylor, with Richard Burton directing. They were unable to do it; then the part was offered to Natalie. There were twelve screenwriters before a script emerged crediting Francis Ford Coppola, Fred Coe and Edith Sommer. Several directors were tentatively involved, including John Huston and John Frankenheimer, but by the time the film had been cast no director had been signed.

Sydney Pollack, whose first directorial effort *The Slender Thread* was being well received, was under consideration. He feels that Redford, a friend since their acting stint in *War Hunt*, put in a good word for him. "He probably said, 'Well, for what it's worth, I know him and I like him and I think he's a good director.' I don't think he'd do anything beyond that because he would have felt it was unprofessional. But he came to me and we talked about it and he said, 'I sure hope you do it because we're really in trouble, and it's a crummy script.' "

Pollack was chosen, and he was somewhat nervous about directing Redford. "My last relationship working with him was two actors talking on a set. Now I was going to be telling him what to do and I thought, This is gonna be rather weird. But it was O.K. Right away there was a tone struck which has remained constant in all our work: a nice mixture between a director and an actor and the odd couple. Oh, we argued like crazy on the set. He'd say, 'Now wait a minute Pollack, you're way off on this' and I'd say, 'Now don't tell me how to do things!' The first time he got personal with me on the set I really was too insecure to handle it very well because I was nervous. It was a big cast on location and Natalie was a very big star at the time. When he'd say, 'No, no, I think I should do it this way,' I'd stop and look around to see if anybody had heard him say that. I thought, God! There goes my image as a director! But of course, it was just the way we worked together."

The production was fraught with difficulties. Twelve screenwriters had not produced a script Pollack found workable, and it was up to him to make sense of

With Mary Badham

Redford and Natalie confer with director Sydney Pollack on location in Louisiana

the numerous versions. "I ended up with a pair of scissors and a staple gun putting together the script from two pages of that one and two pages of this one." Redford was unhappy about the intrusions of producer Ray Stark. "He kept trying to change things, seldom for the better."

When Tennessee Williams read the final shooting script, he asked that his name be disassociated from the film. It wasn't, but Williams was not emphasized in the ad campaign.

During location filming in Bay St. Louis, Mississippi and New Orleans, the crew encountered one problem after another. Redford came down with a fever and was in bed for several days. The people of Bay St. Louis didn't want a film made in their town and circulated a petition to drive the crew out, which the mayor unsuccessfully tried to do. One woman pushed a cameraman off the sidewalk in front of her French Quarter apartment and screamed, "I'm clean living and I'll have no part of a dirty Tennessee Williams movie around my property!"

Charles Bronson, playing a railroad man being laid off by Redford and competing for Alva's affection, complained to Pollack that not enough attention was being paid to his role. "It's a terrific role I'm playing because it could be kind of like a triangle," Bronson told Pollack. "He made sense in a way," Pollack says. "But I couldn't deal with it. I couldn't re-write the part and make it bigger. And the least of my worries at this point was Charlie Bronson's character. My essential concentration was on Natalie. And I didn't see much between Bob and Charlie. Their scenes together were mostly silent. There were a lot of evil looks that passed back and forth but that's all really."

Considering the production problems and so little script help (Redford says, "We would end up improvising, just making things up as we went along, hoping they'd add up to something."), the film and Redford's performance are remarkably successful. His characterization in *This Property is Condemned* is a strong and subtly refined one. As with his three previous films, Redford's notices were better than the movie's.

After three "Hollywood" movies, Robert Redford wasn't sure he wanted to remain an actor. He was the possessor of a ream of favorable reviews and was called the hottest new actor in movies. He was deluged by a storm of movie offers.

But, unlike most actors in the same position, Redford wasn't pleased. "Things seemed unreal," he says. "I wanted to take a break and take it easy for a while." So he packed up Lola, Shauna and Jamie and took off for a small village in Spain, where the Redfords lived for several months until tourists discovered the spot. They then moved to Crete. "I was trying to

find some parts of Europe that were still European, not Americanized. It's not easy to do anymore."

After six months, Redford returned in order to honor a commitment to do the film version of *Barefoot in the Park*.

REVIEWS

"As soggy, sentimental a story of a po' little white-trash gal as ever oozed from the pen of Tennessee Williams or out of the veins of script writers in Hollywood is pictured in Technicolor in Seven Arts' *This Property is Condemned*, which opened yesterday at the Festival and Victoria. And as pretty, bright-eyed and incongruous a specimen of the breed as ever nibbled a piece of Southern fried chicken is presented in it by Natalie Wood.

"But unfortunately, the script (has) so clearly synthesized and overdrawn the sterling qualities of this young woman and made the railroad man of Mr. Redford so pure—such a glowing amalgamation of nobility and gullibility--that the two of them in this cheap environment are wholly implausible."

BOSLEY CROWTHER,
The New York Times

"*This Property is Condemned* . . . has in its favor a technically outstanding production. It moves with all the grace and facility that veteran cameraman James Wong Howe brings to his profession. The stars, while basking in living color, are consistently good. Miss Wood, who is exquisitely photographed, more than meets the demands of an inadequate role. Redford can't help but succeed in the romantic leading man category."

KATHLEEN CARROLL,
New York Daily News

"The picture probably deserves a degree of criticism at the highest level, for it does have a Hollywood gloss laid on the Tennessee Williams view of Southern scene and personnel. And one doubts that Tennessee would have produced such a richness of upsy-downsy plotting.

"On the other hand, the mother, played by Kate Reid, is uncommonly strong, and Robert Redford is a fine and sturdy stranger. . . ."

ARCHER WINSTEN,
New York Post

"*This Property is Condemned* is a handsomely mounted, well-acted Depression era drama . . . adult

With Mary Badham, Redford gives some ruffians a piece of his ice cream cone

without being sensational, and touching without being maudlin. Redford, top-featured, should make a significant leap to stardom via his outstanding performance herein, as the railroad efficiency expert sent to town to lay off most of the crew. Plot-wise, the role is thankless and heavy, but Redford, through voice, expression and movement—total acting—makes the character sympathetic and rounded with depth and feeling, including a flair for light comedy. Under the excellent and sensitive direction of Sydney Pollack, Redford's eventual romantic involvement with Miss Wood illuminates his character as well as hers."

MURF.,
Variety

"Somewhere in the middle of this horrendous soap opera, Robert Redford tells an oriental parable that sort of describes what happened to Williams and his original play when the script writers got through with it. 'A man takes a drink,' said Redford, 'then the drink takes a drink, then the drink takes the man.' . . .

Redford is too good for the movie. So is the photography of James Wong Howe, who imbues the most absurd situations with a glamor and poetic reality they don't deserve."

JOSEPH GELMIS,
Newsday

"There are some dead spots—notably, a scene in an abandoned railroad car in which Robert Redford, as Alva's beau, flats his lines in the awful, self-doubting way of an actor falling out of his part . . . but the main problem throughout the film is Natalie Wood. The trouble is that it takes a very strong, assured actress to play someone so false and nervous without calling the poise of her own performance into question, and Miss Wood seems always on the verge of missing a note . . . Miss Wood actually does make it through all right, and the film survives. But barely."

The New Yorker

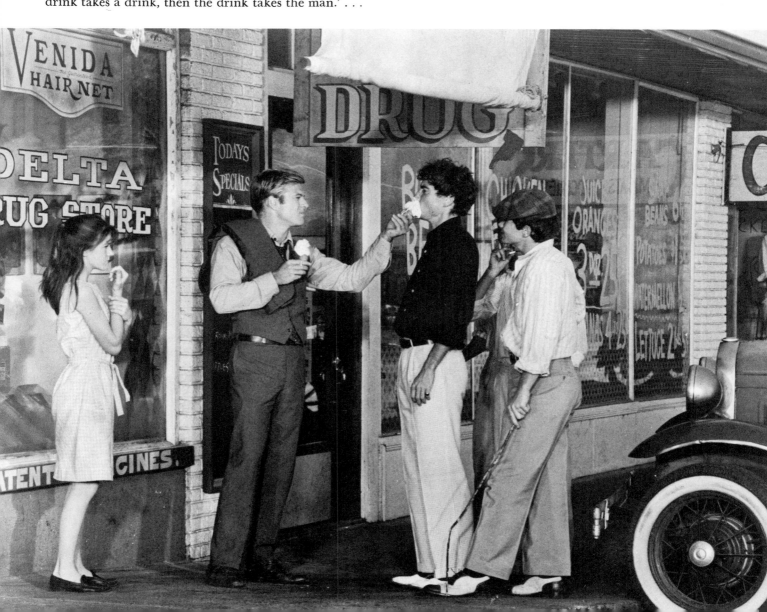

The men Owen has laid off
gang up on him

Alva and Owen find them-
selves falling in love

Newlyweds Paul and Corie Bratter take a hansom cab ride

BAREFOOT IN THE PARK

A Paramount Release (1967). In Technicolor. 106 minutes.

CAST

Paul Bratter, Robert Redford; *Corie Bratter,* Jane Fonda; *Victor Velasco,* Charles Boyer; *Mrs. Banks,* Mildred Natwick; *Telephone Man,* Herbert Edelman; *Delivery Man,* James Stone; *Frank,* Ted Hartley; *Aunt Harriet,* Mabel Albertson; *Restaurant Proprietor,* Fritz Feld.

CREDITS

Produced by Hal Wallis; *Associate Producers:* Neil Simon, Paul Nathan; *Directed by* Gene Saks; *Screenplay by* Neil Simon, *based on his play; Photography by* Joseph La Shelle; *Edited by* William A. Lyon; *Costumes by* Edith Head.

Barefoot—and drunk—in the park

After getting up those stairs with
Mildred Natwick

Redford and Fonda mug for the camera

SYNOPSIS

Corie and Paul Bratter are newlyweds living in a run-down five-floor walkup in New York's Greenwich Village. Free-wheeling Corie is delighted by the "possibilities" of the place, but reserved lawyer Paul is skeptical about the lack of heat and hole in the skylight. Equally unsure of the wisdom of living in the place is Corie's mother, Mrs. Banks, who quickly invites the couple to dinner at her place the following Friday.

Paul is upset too about the kookie tenants in the building, one of whom, Velasco, is known as the "Bluebeard of East 10th Street." In the middle of the night, Corie is awakened by Velasco, who has to go through their apartment to get to his, from which he has been evicted. Corie is enchanted by this oddball, and thinks she can use him to make her mother and husband more fun-loving. She suggests dinner on Friday night.

Mrs. Banks is horrified by the blind date, and when Velasco takes them to Staten Island for an Albanian dinner, she and Paul are green from the ferry ride and the weird dishes. Velasco offers to take Mrs. Banks home to New Jersey, and announces, "Contact us at the National Hotel in Mexico City if you don't hear from us in a week!" Mrs. Banks promises to call Corie in the morning—from her home.

Corie and Paul fight when she accuses him of never letting himself go. Like the time he refused to go barefoot in the park. Paul retorts it was seventeen degrees and wet. Corie is unconvinced and tells him she wants a divorce.

Mrs. Banks tells Corie she fell on the ice leaving the apartment building and had to spend the night in Velasco's apartment. Corie is conscience-stricken about what trouble she has caused her mother. But Mrs. Banks finds the whole situation amusing and develops a tenderness for Velasco, from whom she accepts a dinner invitation. She also tells Corie to make up with Paul.

Corie finds her husband barefoot, and drunk, in the park. He vows to become a nut. She tells him he doesn't have to, but he climbs out on the building roof ledge, precariously holding on. Corie tells him to stay where he is until she gets there.

Redford was surprised by the offer to do the film version of *Barefoot in the Park*. He had been overlooked for the film version of *Sunday in New York* (the three leads went to Cliff Robertson, Rod Taylor and Jane Fonda) and Redford expected the same to happen with *Barefoot*: "I thought it was the rule for the Broadway actors to be ignored for the film."

He wasn't at all sure he wanted to do it. "I hate to repeat myself." But just as the play had followed

With Jane Fonda, Mildred Natwick and Charles Boyer

several Broadway flops and ignited Redford's career, it was clear that the film's chances for success were quite good. So Redford accepted the assignment. Mildred Natwick would be repeating her Broadway characterization as well, but the Corie Bratter role went to Jane Fonda.

The filming in New York went well. There were few script problems (Neil Simon wrote the screenplay) and the characterizations were pretty well established by the show's four-year run on Broadway. The director, Gene Saks (husband of Bea Arthur of TV's *Maude*), recalls several things about Redford which have stuck with him. The character was not a favorite of his," says Saks. "He hated wearing a blue suit, button down collar and tie all day. He seemed anxious that people on the set know that he wasn't really like that character. He would wear a black western hat and cowboy boots around the set when he wasn't on camera." (A famous publicity still for the film shows Redford in that outfit, with his shoelaces untied.)

Bob's enjoyment of fast driving took its toll on Saks, who went for a wild ride one night and wished he hadn't. "I was terrified, but Bob was having a great time. I was sure the jig was up for both of us. After that, I went out of my way not to ride with him—anywhere—again."

Redford and Fonda, who worked together much more in this film than in *The Chase*, became close friends during the filming. Bob, far more familiar with the story than Jane, helped her find the right mixture of elements to make her performance work.

The film, like the play, opened to rave reviews and became the first commercially successful Redford movie. Among those clamoring for Redford's services after *Barefoot* was Mike Nichols, who wanted badly to work with Redford again.

Although he couldn't convince Bob to do *Virginia Woolf*, Nichols thought he might be good for the role of *The Graduate*. Redford read the script and liked it. He and Nichols batted the idea around for a while. "I never offered him the part, really, and he never said he would do it," says Nichols. "It was all very exploratory. Bob thought he wouldn't *look* the part, so we filmed a scene to see how it would come off on film.

"Once we saw the screen test," Nichols goes on, "we realized Bob was wrong for the part. My strongest reaction was that no one would believe that Redford was a guy who would have any difficulty with women —and that was a big part of the script. Bob agreed with me, and he wasn't happy. He complained that he might be stuck all his life playing good-looking golden boys."

REVIEWS

"*Barefoot in the Park* is the kind of picture that fills Radio City Music Hall with happy customers for weeks and weeks. The hilarious comedy . . . comes off better on the screen than on the stage. This is the best compliment that could be paid to the film—the original has been a hit since October 23, 1963. The improvement in the screen version can be attributed to the camera that moves the action out of a one-set presentation, showing incidents and sights around New York only referred to in the play. Each performance is a gem."

KATHLEEN CARROLL,
New York Daily News

". . . The amount of fun writer Neil Simon can wring out of these rather tired situations is astounding. The cast is a big help. Fonda and Redford work together wonderfully. Mildred Natwick is as appealing as she has ever been, perhaps more so, and Boyer pumps up the gusto."

ARCHER WINSTEN,
New York Post

"If it's romantic farce you delight in—old-fashioned romantic farce loaded with incongruities and snappy verbal gags—then you should find the movie version of *Barefoot in the Park* to your taste . . . But if you are for a certain measure of intelligence and plausibility in what is presumed to be a takeout of what might happen to reckless newlyweds today, if you expect a wisp of logic in the make-up of comic characters which is, after all, what makes them funny, instead of sheer gagging it up, then beware.

"Much of the early part of the picture, including a prologue honeymoon in the Plaza Hotel, is taken up with scenes of Miss Fonda osculating and running around in scanty attire. So voracious is her ardor, it's no wonder that Mr. Redford, who originated the role of the husband in the stage play and seemed reasonably relaxed in it, plays most of his scenes in a state of tenuous terror, as though fearful of being attacked —all of which makes one wonder how such a normal and nervous fellow could ever have got himself hooked up with this Kookie Kid."

BOSLEY CROWTHER,
The New York Times

"*Barefoot in the Park* is one howl of a picture . . . a thoroughly entertaining comedy delight about a young marriage . . . Redford is an outstanding actor, particularly adept in light comedy, whose performance herein justifies his first position over the title. He should have a successful film career for decades, the logical follow-up to Cary Grant . . . Miss Fonda is excellent."

MURF.,
Variety

Filming at the Albanian restaurant on Staten Island (with Jane Fonda, Mildred Natwick and Charles Boyer)

Filming on location in New York with Jane Fonda

With Paul Newman

BUTCH CASSIDY AND THE SUNDANCE KID

A 20th Century-Fox Release of a Campanile Production (1969). In Panavision and DeLuxe Color. 110 minutes. Rated PG.

CAST

Butch Cassidy, Paul Newman; *The Sundance Kid*, Robert Redford; *Etta Place*, Katharine Ross; *Percy Garris*, Strother Martin; *Bike Salesman*, Henry Jones; *Sheriff Bledsoe*, Jeff Corey; *Woodcock*, George Furth; *Agnes*, Cloris Leachman; *Harvey Logan*, Ted Cassidy; *Marshal*, Kenneth Mars; *Macon*, Donnelly Rhodes; *Large Woman*, Jody Gilbert; *News Carver*, Timothy Scott; *Fireman*, Don Keefer; *Flat Nose Curry*, Charles Dierkop; *Bank Manager*, Francisco Cordova; *Photographer*, Nelson Olmstead; *Card Player #1*, Paul Bryar; *Card Player #2*, Sam Elliott; *Bank Teller*, Charles Akins; *Tiffany's Salesman*, Eric Sinclair.

CREDITS

Executive Producer: Paul Monash; *Produced by* John Foreman; *Directed by* George Roy Hill; *Written by* William Goldman; *Music Composed and Conducted by* Burt Bacharach; *"Raindrops Keep Falling on My Head" Lyrics and Music by* Hal David and Burt Bacharach; *Sung by* B. J. Thomas; *Photography by* Conrad Hall, A.S.C.; *Costumes by* Edith Head; *Art Direction by* Jack Martin Smith, Philip Jefferies; *Edited by* John C. Howard, Richard C. Meyer, A.C.E.; *Assistant Director,* Steven Bernhardt; *Special Still Photography by* Lawrence Schiller.

Redford as the Sundance Kid

Redford, Katharine Ross and Newman share a laugh during filming in Bolivia

SYNOPSIS

Butch Cassidy joins his sidekick, the Sundance Kid, in Macon's saloon, where Sundance has just been accused by Macon of cheating at blackjack. Macon takes back the charge when he realizes that the pair are the leaders of the infamous Hole-in-the-Wall gang. As they leave, Macon asks Sundance if he is really as fast on the draw as they say—and Sundance answers by instantly shooting off Macon's gunbelt.

As the pair ride back to their mountain retreat, Butch suggests they give up their robberies in the West and go South of the border to Bolivia, where they'd have easy pickings of gold, tin and silver mines. When they get to the Hole-in-the-Wall, they find that Logan has decided to take over the Gang from Butch. But Butch quickly puts down the revolt with a swift kick.

The Gang plans to rob a Union Pacific train twice —once going and once on the return trip. They assume the railroad would never suspect that the robbers would hit the same train twice and figure that the train on the return run will be loaded with money. After the first robbery, Butch goes to the local brothel and Sundance visits his girlfriend Etta Place, who always waits for his return.

The second robbery is broken up by a second train sent by the company filled with a posse. Butch and Sundance keep one step ahead of their pursuers, but are unable to elude them until they jump from a steep cliff into a raging mountain stream. With Etta's help and company, they go to Bolivia where they continue their illegal exploits until they're finally cornered. Up to the last minute, as shots ring out around them, Butch plans a trip to Australia for their future exploits.

If the huge commercial success of *Barefoot in the Park* made Redford an actor to be reckoned with in Hollywood, it also helped establish an image for him which he hated and which was contrary to his true personality. He wasn't a stuffy, Eastern establishment Wall Street lawyer whose idea of the great outdoors is Central Park. But his performance in *Barefoot* was so good, his characterization so real, that this was the impression many Hollywood bigwigs had of him. And this image almost cost him the role that finally was to establish him as a first-rank star.

Butch Cassidy and the Sundance Kid was the brain-child of writer William Goldman, who spent six years researching the lives of the two bandits who ran roughshod over the American Southwest at the turn of the century. The screenplay, which Goldman sold to 20th Century-Fox for a record $400,000, was a delightful mix of action, humor, pathos and tragedy. It presented the outlaws as human beings, complete with foibles, senses of humor and self-doubts. "I

originally wrote the script with Jack Lemmon in mind for Butch and Paul Newman for Sundance," says Goldman. "I had seen Lemmon in the film *Cowboy* and Newman in *Billy the Kid* and I thought they'd be great together."

But Richard Zanuck, the head of 20th Century-Fox, had other ideas. He wanted two superstars in the roles, and offered the Butch role to Steve McQueen and the Sundance part to Paul Newman. Both tentatively agreed, and it was this package which was offered to George Roy Hill, a relatively new director best known for *Thoroughly Modern Millie* and *Hawaii*.

Hill had different ideas about the casting and his disagreement with Zanuck resulted in months of haggling and the near-suspension of the production. Hill saw Newman as Butch, and set out to convince Paul. "He wasn't confident he could do it," says Hill. "He saw it as a comic part and said to me, 'I just proved to myself I can't play comedy doing *The Secret War of Harry Frigg*.' But I told him it wasn't a comic part. Butch was a totally straight guy in sometimes comic situations."

Steve McQueen, Hill thought, wasn't right for either part, but especially not Butch. Once McQueen learned that Newman was considering playing Butch and that, no matter what part he played, Newman wanted top billing, McQueen bowed out. At this point Hill didn't give a second thought to who should play opposite Newman. He wanted Robert Redford. "I had read Bob for a part in *Period of Adjustment*, my first film, in 1962. I thought he was a very rugged guy, quite physical, with a great deal of underlying warmth. After seeing him in *Sunday in New York*, I knew he could handle comic situations, and that's exactly what I needed. I decided that if Newman wasn't going to play Butch, then Redford was right for it."

Hill got together with Redford in New York and asked him if he could play Butch. "Sure I can play Butch," Redford replied, "But I'd be better as Sundance." As the evening progressed, Hill became persuaded. "Finally," he says, "I was convinced that it had to be Newman as Butch and Redford as Sundance."

Newman wasn't sure. He told Hill, "Redford's a Wall Street lawyer type. Are you sure he's right for this?" Hill assured him Redford was perfect, and Newman agreed to remain neutral. "He hates to get involved in those things anyway," says Hill. Goldman was at first opposed, but then changed his mind. The only people left to convince now were Zanuck and the film's producers, Paul Monash and John Foreman. It wasn't easy.

"Zanuck thought of Redford as some kind of oddball," remembers Hill. "He said to me, 'Redford's not the outdoors type. And besides, he's been up to bat a couple of times and hasn't made it.' So Zanuck decided that Marlon Brando should play Sundance. There was a big meeting in his office with Monash, Foreman, me and a couple of other guys. Zanuck stood at his desk and said 'I think Brando should play Sundance. What do you guys think?' And he went down the line, and you heard 'Brando,' 'Brando,' 'Brando,' 'Brando.' Then he got to me and I said 'Redford.' Everyone looked at me as though I was out of my skull. They decided to go ahead and contact Brando, and all the time I was holding out. I was scared to death of Brando in the first place, and I didn't think he was right for the part. But they were proceeding, and Paul said Brando was eager to do it, so I stopped my kicking and screaming and relented.

"Well," Hill goes on, "Brando was nowhere to be found. For two weeks we looked for him. Finally we gave up when Elia Kazan called and asked if *we* knew where he was because he wanted to talk to him about *The Arrangement*. Well, we figured if *Kazan* couldn't find him, what chance did we have? I thought it was pretty odd for a guy who was *anxious* to play a role."

Thus, the scene in Zanuck's office was repeated, this time with everyone agreeing that Warren Beatty should play Sundance—except Hill. "At this point they were ready to kill me," he says. "They figured I had a hang-up about Redford—was related to him or something. But I continued to hold out. Finally Zanuck got angry and said he would cancel the production rather than use Redford. He then called Beatty and offered him the part."

At this point, Hill decided to pull out all the stops. "I called Paul and told him I thought Zanuck was making a mistake, that Redford was the right guy for this part. I asked him to do me a favor and back Redford. He called Zanuck and stated very forcefully that Redford was the man he wanted. Goldman sent a six-page telegram asking Zanuck why, if the whole creative team agreed on this, management wouldn't go along? Finally, Zanuck relented and we had Redford."

All this time, Redford was holding out, not accepting other film offers. "I put it out of my mind," says Redford. "I just stayed out of it until somebody told me the deal was made." Hill admired Redford's tenacity. "That takes guts," he says. "Because it must be a hell of a blow to an actor's ego. But Redford is a stubborn son of a bitch. He's a great competitor. Hates to lose!"

Once filming began, any reservations Zanuck had evaporated. "There's no question he's right for the part," Zanuck told Hill. Redford brought to the role just those qualities Hill wanted. "Redford's a leading man, a man's man, strong, terse, sardonic. I think he brought a great deal of his own personality to the part. Bob is a very hard-nosed, independent, private person. And he has a tendency to be very cool on the exterior, and very distant. Yet he has a tremendous warmth underneath it. If you have a cold man playing a potential killer, it's repulsive. Redford was able to play against the underlying warmth and make the character full-bodied. It was exactly what I wanted."

Redford felt totally comfortable in the role. "I had a strange identification with Sundance that I can't quite put my finger on," he says. "There was a time when I was very young that I didn't think it would be so bad to be an outlaw. It sounded pretty good to me. The frontier wouldn't have been a bad place to be in the 1880s, it seemed to me. You didn't turn your back on too many people, but the atmosphere was free and you carved out of it what you could make of it. One reason I liked the script was that it pointed out the fact that a lot of those people were just kids, doing what they did—robbing banks, holding up trains—as much for the sheer fun of it as anything else."

Redford and Newman hit it off immediately. "They're both self-aware men with modern sensibilities," says Hill. "It was a rare kind of relationship between those two guys, on and off the set. There was continued bantering. They were very fond of each other."

Their acting styles conflicted, however, and that caused Redford some impatience. As Hill explains it, "Redford doesn't like to talk about a scene. If I say, 'Let's do the scene this way,' he'll say, 'Yeah, good, let's try it.' Paul will talk it to death. His security as an actor comes from getting the scene straight in his head intellectually. Redford gets very impatient, but he usually deferred to Paul's style."

"Paul really is a good guy," says Redford, "I really like him. Otherwise I would have balked at the whole rehearsal thing. I believe rehearsal cuts into the spontaneity of what you're doing, and spontaneity is vitally important in films, since films are essentially about capturing life as it happens. That's the illusion they try to create, anyway. But I rehearsed. Newman was calling the shots so I rehearsed."

Despite this basic conflict between the two stars, a tremendous spirit of fun permeated the *Butch Cassidy* filming. There was a great deal of ribbing, joking and challenging going on among Newman, Redford and Hill. Redford feigns anger as he says, "I really *worked* on the being-fast-with-the-gun business, and every time I'd screw one up, Hill would be over there with his hand over his mouth, going, 'Heh, heh, heh, what's the matter, Redford?' He was always telling me to be careful not to shoot myself in the foot." Hill admits he enjoyed the times Redford "screwed up." "My favorite image of him in the picture," he says, "is

the expression on his face when he messed up one of the first scenes we shot. He was supposed to jump off the train they were robbing and then, while it rolled to a stop, give an arm signal to the others and run back to the door of the payroll car. Well, Redford works so *physically*, and he was so concerned with this arm wave he was doing and the graceful way he was running and stopped and turning, that he didn't notice that the train had rolled right past him. When he looked up and didn't see it, and looked around for where it had gone, the expression on his face was incredible—I literally couldn't talk for five minutes. I tried every way possible to use that piece of film in the picture, but I just couldn't get it in."

Newman used to love riding Redford about his constant lateness. "You know, Redford's left-handed," Newman says. "I wanted to change the name of the picture to *Waiting for Lefty*."

But by far the most fun were the hoaxes these three grown-up kids used to play on each other. "I like a caper," says Redford. "My favorite kind is the set-up." And Redford was the victim of a beauty dreamed up by Hill. After seeing the director practicing fencing, Redford started to tease him. "The next thing I knew, this clumsy oaf—who never exercises at anything except lifting a whiskey glass—challenged me to a fencing match for a hundred dollars. I watched him working out with his assistant, Bob Crawford, and when I saw

Butch and the Kid on the run

Redford practices "The quick-on-the-draw stuff"

how inept he was, I figured I didn't even have to train."

When the time of the match came, Hill came hobbling over and told Redford he'd sprained his ankle. Redford was gleeful. "Hill, you blew it! You really blew it!" And Hill said, "Sure, take the money. If you don't mind winning by default, take it." "I thought it over," says Redford, "and it didn't seem right, so I offered to postponed the match. Hill gets charitable about the whole thing and offers to pick a stand in. I knew I had him now, because there wasn't a chance he'd pick a winner. He went down the whole crew and couldn't find a taker. Finally he came to Bob Crawford. He was a pretty young kid, and he hadn't looked much better than Hill when I watched them work out, so I didn't think much of the choice. But as soon as the match began, I knew I'd been had. That kid turned out to be a Junior Olympic champion fencer!"

Newman and Redford plotted revenge by challenging Hill to a race. As Hill explains it, "I was going to fly my biplane, Newman was driving his Volks, which has a Porsche engine, and Redford was driving his Porsche. We figured the time was about equal because I had to re-fuel somewhere. What Newman planned to do, we found out later, was to charter a goddamned *transport* plane, drive the Volks inside, fly to Provo or wherever the hell it was, land, idle the engine, and sit there drinking beer while we screwed around trying to get there. But *Redford* was so goddamned serious about it that finally I had to call it off. It was hunting season, see, and I was really afraid that he'd kill himself, or some damned hunters, trying to *win!*"

Paul Newman looks at all this as more than just tomfoolery. In fact, he thinks it was all part of Hill's strategy as a director. "George has such an uncanny sense of story and character that there's a reason for *everything* the wily bastard does. With the little con games, he was effectively getting Redford and me into the spirit of the picaresque guys we were playing."

Whatever the reasons, Hill's success with *Butch Cassidy* was readily evident upon its release in late 1969. The film was an instant blockbuster, and the attention given Redford was massive. Story after story in magazines and newspapers proclaimed him an "overnight sensation."

He made the cover of *Life* and this was his first real taste of fame. "I'd walk down the street and see my face staring out at me from newsstand after newsstand and I just wanted to go someplace and hide." There *wasn't* anyplace for Redford to hide, though. From this point on, he was of that singular breed: a Hollywood superstar.

Butch and the Kid comfort Etta

The Hole-in-the-Wall Gang

REVIEWS

"*Butch Cassidy and the Sundance Kid* . . . is a very nice film. It is a nearly perfect film. Visually attractive, comfortably humorous, it cannot fail to please . . . The stars are attractive, the direction imaginative but not too way out . . . Everyone will love it. One can sit through it with enjoyment and recommend it to one's friends as a socially acceptable way to spend an evening. But . . . it will not stir any buried emotions. It will not drag the hidden stores of laughter from the gut, or tweak with pain the drugged regions of the soul, or break loose the dammed channels of the mind.

"Newman and Redford are excellent. With perfect comic timing, they sheepishly admit inadequacies of character which they then surmount. Redford gets to one a little more, probably because he is a little more vibrant and vulgar and a little less well known. But Newman's eyes are very, very blue.

"I enjoyed it very much but I did not care when they died. I wanted to."

BRIDGET BYRNE,
Los Angeles Times

". . . Much of *Butch Cassidy and the Sundance Kid* is very funny in a strictly contemporary way—the last exuberant word on movies about men of the mythic American West who have outlived their day . . . There are some bothersome technical things about the movie (the camera is all zoom, zoom, zoom) but the over-all production is very handsome, and the performances fine, especially Newman, Redford and Miss Ross, who must be broadly funny and straight, almost simultaneously. They succeed, even if the movie does not."

VINCENT CANBY,
The New York Times

"We expect Paul to be completely at home in Westerns. And it was a delightful surprise to see Robert take to the tough, tobacco-chewing outlaw as if he'd played Westerns before he became an accomplished stage and screen comedian."

WANDA HALE,
New York Daily News

". . . Robert Redford is quite superb, proceeding effortlessly from a complete control of character which ensures that every emphasis is telling . . ."

DEREK PROUSE,
London Sunday Times

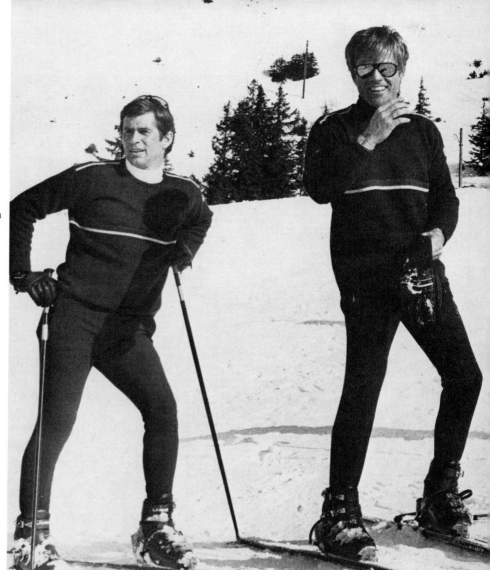

With Jim McMullen

Arriving in Grenoble (with Gene Hackman)

With Camilla Sparv

DOWNHILL RACER

A Paramount Release of a Wildwood International Picture (1969). In Technicolor. 101 minutes. Rated M.

CAST

David Chappellet, Robert Redford; *Eugene Claire,* Gene Hackman; *Carole Stahl,* Camilla Sparv; *Machet,* Karl Michael Vogler; *Creech,* Jim McMullan; *Brumm,* Christian Doermer; *American Newspaperwoman,* Kathleen Crowley; *Mayo,* Dabney Coleman; *D.K.,* Timothy Kirk; *Kipsmith,* Oren Stevens; *Engel,* Jerry Dexter; *David's father,* Walter Stroud; *Lena,* Carole Carle; *Devore,* Rip McManus; *Tommy,* Joe Jay Jalbert; *Stiles,* Tom J. Kirk; *Gabriel,* Robin Hutton-Potts; *Meier,* Heini Schuler; *Boyriven,* Peter Rohr; *Hinsch,* Arnold Alpiger; *Haas,* Eddie Waldburger; *Istel,* Marco Walli.

CREDITS

Produced by Richard Gregson; *Directed by* Michael Ritchie; *Screenplay by* James Salter; *Based on "The Downhill Racers" by* Oakley Hall; *Photography by* Brian Probyn; *Production Manager:* Walter Coblenz; *Assistant Director:* Kip Gowans; *Art Direction by* Ian Whittaker.

SYNOPSIS

The American ski team is in Switzerland for the Olympic trials. Their top skier is hurt, and coach Eugene Clair sends for two replacements, D.K. Bryan and David Chappellet. Chappellet is a tough, undisciplined loner from Colorado, a man who has never had much more than his skis to rely on.

After refusing to run his first race because he has been put in the 88th starting position, making it impossible for him to do well, Chappellet puts in a superb performance in the next big race, eclipsing the team's star, Johnny Creech. At a postrace party, stars from other countries' teams are present, but the newsmen crowd around David. He is intent on a beautiful girl, Carole, who is there with her boss, ski manufacturer Machet.

After several more races, the season ends badly for the Americans and David returns home to Colorado. His father welcomes him but says nothing, denying David the words of praise he had hoped for.

The following season, David has worked his way up to being seeded twentieth, and he wins his first race. During another, he falls, but Creech comes in second.

David gets to know Carole, and neglects a practice run to be with her. Later, David wins a fabulous victory for the Americans. But in the next race, he falls again, and the headlines go to Creech. David and Carole spend more and more time together. When the season ends in glory for the Americans, all eyes are upon them for the next year's Olympics.

David's preoccupation with the upcoming races and his self-centered personality upset Carole, and she refuses to spend Christmas with him. Later, during the pre-Olympics, they meet by chance in a club. But it is too late for them to make it together and they realize it.

In the last pre-Olympic race, David does brilliantly in the men's downhill. He is in first place, but just as it seems that he has won a gold medal, an un-heralded skier is reported to be coming close to David's time. Just as it seems that he will beat David, he falls—and the medal is David's. Realizing how close he was to defeat, and that he must live for himself and for the present, David savors his moment of triumph.

Before Redford had even been considered for *Butch Cassidy,* he had been trying to get Paramount Pictures to finance an independent venture of his about an Olympic skiing athlete. They asked him to film *The Ski Bum,* but that wasn't the kind of movie he had in mind. "I wanted to make a film that was pure and simple about a racer."

He got in touch with writer James Salter and asked him to come up with a script. Since Paramount had

just signed a deal with Roman Polanski, they offered him the direction and he agreed. Everything was proceeding smoothly. Then the problems began.

Redford was supposed to begin filming a western for Paramount called *Blue.* But unbeknownst to him, the script was changed. When he read it, he realized the movie wasn't good and felt that he had no obligation to do the film because it wasn't the same one he had agreed to make. He told Paramount he had no intention of showing up for filming, and Paramount sued him for several hundred thousand dollars.

"On top of that," Redford says, "Polanski was over budget on *Rosemary's Baby* and the whole thing started to fumble and fall. Then when they got the treatment from Salter, Paramount hated it! Salter writes for film and not for the paper for people to read. Paramount dropped the project. But I guarantee you if Polanski and I had been in real tight with them, they wouldn't have dropped it. But at that time, they had machine gun turrets set up on that lot for me."

It may have been a stroke of luck for Redford, actually, that the studio backed out. They didn't understand what he was trying to do. "It wasn't supposed to be a picture about skiing," says Redford, "although the studio never got that through their heads." They wanted him to use *The Downhill Racers,* a novel by Oakley Hall, which Redford didn't want because "it's really an *après*-ski book. I wanted this movie to be the portrait of an athlete, a certain kind of person in American society."

Redford felt strongly about portraying the American athlete as he really was. "I felt I knew the person because of my early life in sports. There came a point when I turned against what it had to offer. The competition itself was exciting but once you stepped outside that arena you saw what you were missing in life. It had annoyed me the way athletes had been portrayed in films. They were always clean-cut, mid-dle-American types who came off the farms and had great wives behind them and great moms and dads. It was a Norman Rockwell depiction of America and that's not the way I saw it. I said, 'What about the athlete who's a creep?' We do tend to tolerate creeps if they win. Who remembers who came in second? I wanted to see that in a film and it only happened to be skiing because I was into it at the time and thought it was something very beautiful and visual that hadn't been dealt with in film before."

Redford decided to produce the package himself, and he and his ex-agent Richard Gregson formed Wildwood Enterprises for that purpose. But he still needed studio money. Once a settlement had been reached in the *Blue* matter, Redford spoke to Charles Bluhdorn, President of Gulf and Western, Paramount's parent company. For fifteen minutes Redford acted out the character he had in mind. Then he told Bluhdorn he could bring the film in under the $3 million budget the studio had originally set. "He thought there was something there," Redford says. Bluhdorn told Redford to get as much footage as he could for as little money as possible, and Redford set out for Grenoble to film actual competition in the Olympics there.

He knew he'd have to have professional skiers for most of the film's action footage. "I'm pretty good on skis," he explains, "but we *had* to shoot the actual Olympic skiers because those few men are the only ones in the world who can race that downhill course authentically. You're skiing eighty miles an hour; one false move and goodbye, Charley. I wanted to show Paramount I could get the footage without spending a lot, so I got the writer, the photographer and some ski-bum assistants over to Grenoble on my own. We were all holed up in one room in this dive by the river. And the French weren't letting people film the Olympics, so we had to use disguises to get by the guards. The photographer was pretty well known, so I fixed him up a hairpiece and a false nose so he could get out on the slopes with his camera. He loved it. The ski bums shot a lot of footage too, but they couldn't get by the officials, so they swiped a sign from a refreshment vendor, put it in their car window, and got through that way. Every night we met at the room to see who was still alive. But we came back with 20,000 feet of film."

Redford finally got a go-ahead from Paramount, with a new budget of $1 million and the stipulation that the title *Downhill Racer* be used. But everything else was up to him. As he puts it, "I inherited the whole enchilada." Redford and Gregson then started to look for a director.

Watching a made-for-TV movie called *The Outsider*, Redford was impressed by Michael Ritchie's direction and offered him that assignment on *Downhill Racer,* even though Ritchie had never directed a feature film before. "I was very flattered to get the call," says Ritchie. "I had known Redford from his earliest days on television—I saw one of the first things he did on TV, *Moment of Fear,* and I'd seen him on Broadway, so I knew he was terrific and somebody I'd like to work with."

While Redford filmed *Butch Cassidy,* Ritchie and Gregson scouted locations in Europe and kept in touch by phone. As soon as Redford finished *Butch,* filming on *Downhill Racer* was set to begin. But there was a problem—Redford injured his knee in a ski-mobile accident. He drove the vehicle over a cliff and decided to stay with it rather than jump clear as it tore downhill. "Pretty soon I was just blasting through

Bob's friend Natalie Wood visits the set

David in training

big powder drifts. I literally flew through the air in this machine. And when it landed, my knee went right into the motor. That cooled me down a little."

It also upset Ritchie. "I was appalled at how I was going to get Redford on skis, because he had a bad limp and this injury was going to take a while to mend. So we shot non-skiing scenes first. If you look closely you'll see he limps somewhat in some of the early scenes. He was enormously frustrated because he wanted to get out on the ski slopes. But by the time

With Camilla Sparv

we got to those segments, Redford was doing a lot of his own skiing."

Which didn't please the studio boys one bit. They wanted Redford's stand-in to do his skiing for him, lest he jeopardize his valuable body. But Redford would have none of it, and there was little the studio could do about it. "We were too far up the mountains for the studio to reach us," he smiles, "so there was really no way they could force me to control whatever it was I was doing. But the question becomes, what is dangerous? I think driving around in Hollywood is dangerous. I think some meetings in some offices are dangerous. I'd rather be on the mountain any day."

It was clear that Ritchie and Redford were in agreement about the kind of look the film should have. As Ritchie puts it, "I wanted this picture to be as gutsy, as realistic, as harsh and as documentary as possible—which would have been very hard to do if our actors had required very precise lighting or camera angles. But we had the advantage of Redford, who is a young, good-looking, rugged guy and doesn't have to be carefully key-lighted or anything like that.

The Olympic Ski Team

As our second lead we had Gene Hackman, who is not concerned about how he looks. As our female lead we had Camilla Sparv who, I am convinced, is impossible to photograph badly. She's just one of those fantastically photogenic women who can be filmed under the worst circumstances and still come out looking beautiful.

"Then, too, we used a lot of real people who had never acted before—people who would have been put ill at ease by an enormous amount of hot lighting equipment, or by being told they had to hit critical marks. I wanted to have a certain freedom, a looseness, the opportunity to shoot rehearsals and use them, the facility to have the camera searching out the action, rather than anticipating it—so that, ultimately, the audience wouldn't be able to tell where the dramatic material left off and the documentary ski footage began."

A great deal of *Downhill Racer* was improvised. A key scene in which Redford blows the horn of Camilla Sparv's car rather than listen to what she has to say (revealing a great deal about the character), was written the night before it was filmed, two and one half months into the filming.

Less important but amusing is Ritchie's story of the scene in Colorado when Redford and a local girl sit in his car and talk after having sex. "It was supposed to be shot outdoors, very pastoral. But the day of the filming, there was a fearful snowstorm. We were behind schedule, so we had to shoot it in the car, using a long lens so you couldn't see the snow swirling outside. After all, it was supposed to be summer!"

Few disagreements arose between Ritchie and Redford, but there was one habit of Bob's that used to get on Mike's nerves. "Bob likes to chew gum in scenes," says Ritchie, "and I don't like that at all. So just as we were ready to roll, Bob would sneak some gum into his mouth and be ready to start chewing. But just as he took his first chomp, I'd always yell 'cut!'"

Once the film was completed, and ready for preview, Redford thought his problems with Paramount would be over. But the worst was yet to come. "We asked Paramount please, because of the nature of the film, let it be known in the papers what was being previewed," says Redford. "None of that old crap about a sneak surprise! Well, we went up to Santa Barbara, that great *liberal stronghold* by the sea with all those *young* folks retired from the East. Those people had come out here to get away from the snow and the last thing they wanted to see was a lot of skiing!

"But one really can't blame Paramount for what ensued; I'd say that damn near half the audience walked out. I just about fainted. Gregson and Natalie Wood and I were sitting in the back and Natalie said, 'I've been through a million of these. I was at one where the whole audience walked out. They threw things at the screen.' I said, 'Could you just be quiet, please,' and slumped down in my seat. I was beginning to wait for that—people throwing things at the screen on their way out.

"After it was over, Bob Evans saddled over and said, 'Gee, I think it played beautifully,'" Redford laughs. "Actually, he was very nice.

"Because of that reaction, you figure there is a possibility the film will not be appreciated," says Redford, with his gift for understatement. "So Gregson, Ritchie and I stayed up all night for two weeks straight. We took out almost all the music. We felt it was more of a movie of natural effects which we had recorded on the slopes. It was a movie that had to be tightened because the pace of the film really was dictated by the subject of skiing."

Despite all these forebodings of disaster, the newly-edited *Downhill Racer* received highly favorable critical reaction. Redford and Ritchie were praised for the film's beauty and realism, and for the refreshingly different view of an American athlete. But, despite the film's excellence, it never reached the audience Redford had hoped for. "It took two years of my life, but it wasn't very successful commercially. Really the films that I've wanted to make and have really been behind haven't made much money. That's the way it is. But you end up with the satisfaction of doing something on film that you have a kind of passion for."

REVIEWS

"*Downhill Racer* . . . is that rare sports film that is shown from the point of view of the sportsman, rather than the spectator or admiring enthusiast. It focuses on those downhill races, on the grim tension that precedes them, the steely exhiliration of them and the exhausted triumph or defeat that follows them . . . Robert Redford, who practically willed the picture into existence out of his own regard for the sport, plays the skier as a very cool and intense young rustic, hell-bent for professional glory and determined to let no one stand in his way. He is not a sympathetic person but, although he nearly becomes a mere function of his own ambition, he is also dumbly aware of the price for victory that must be paid out of his soul . . . *Downhill Racer* is an honest, fresh and bracing film, the best film about an athlete since *This Sporting Life*."

DAVID ELLIOTT,
Chicago Daily News

With Camilla Sparv

"Robert Redford delivers the soundest performance of his movie career as an egocentric, thin-skinned competitor from the backwoods of Colorado . . . The chills, spills and exacting discipline of the sport are captured by brilliant action photography and by the presence in supporting roles of several first-rank professional skiers. Redford, to his credit—and to the credit of freshman director Michael Ritchie, a promising recruit from television—fits easily into this fast company and never compromises the truth of his role by playing for sympathy. He comes on tough, ambitious, none too bright but instinctively shrewd . . . "

Playboy

"The reason *Downhill Racer* at the Baronet is so good is that a young movie star, Robert Redford, had been a good athlete in college, which happened to be in Colorado, where he was belatedly bitten by the ski bug . . . It's very difficult for one who is fascinated by skiing, like this reviewer, to know the degree of interest this film will inspire in the non-skier. The truth is in the picture, and the human factors are honestly portrayed, and very well. The monstrous thrill of the DH comes to you in terms of blurred speed and rushing sound. Redford's performance, in case you haven't been reading between the lines, is a beauty."

ARCHER WINSTEN,
New York Post

"Robert Redford seems to have been the guiding spirit and driving force behind this movie, and so he is more responsible for the overall tone of the movie than most movie stars ever are. And obviously he must feel that athletes are in some measure spiritually impoverished instruments of other peoples' vicarious experiences. Redford is, despite his distractingly good looks, an accomplished actor with the ability to suggest feelings between his lines and his silences. But I can't help feeling that he is looking down on sports in a fakey-humanistic manner for the edification of the great silent majority of armchair athletes who would like to believe that physical grace can exist only in a vacuum."

ANDREW SARRIS,
The Village Voice

As Sheriff Cooper

TELL THEM WILLIE BOY IS HERE

A Universal Pictures Release of a Jennings Lang Presentation (1969). In Panavision and Technicolor. 98 minutes. Rated GP.

CAST

Cooper, Robert Redford; *Lola,* Katharine Ross; *Willie,* Robert Blake; *Liz,* Susan Clark; *Calvert,* Barry Sullivan; *Hacker,* John Vernon; *Benby,* Charles Aidman; *Wilson,* Charles McGraw; *Finney,* Shelly Novack; *Newcombe,* Robert Lipton.

CREDITS

Produced by Philip A. Waxman; *Written and Directed by* Abraham Polonsky; *Based on the novel "Willie Boy" by* Harry Lawton; *Photography:* Conrad Hall, A.S.C.; *Art Direction by* Alexander Golitzen, Henry Bumstead; *Assistant Director:* Joseph Kenny; *Edited by* Melvin Shapiro; *Costumes by* Edith Head; *Music by* Dave Grusin.

SYNOPSIS

Willie Boy, a Paiute Indian working as a cow-puncher, returns to Banning, California in 1909 to claim Lola Boniface as his bride. Her father, Old Mike, is against the marriage and tries to prevent them from leaving. During the ensuing fight, Willie Boy shoots Old Mike. Tribal custom terms Willie's action a "marriage by capture." He and Lola flee on foot, with few supplies, because the murder has taken place on white man's land.

The reservation superintendent, Dr. Elizabeth Arnold, urges Christopher Cooper, Under Sheriff of Banning, to capture the pair and bring Lola back. Coop enlists rancher Ray Calvert and cowhand Charlie Newcombe for the capture, which they're convinced will be easy. But Willie Boy, familiar with the trail, eludes them and Coop decides to give up the search to serve as a bodyguard to President Taft, who is visiting. Calvert and Newcombe carry on the pursuit, and Willie fires at them, hitting Calvert. The posse panics and wires Sheriff Wilson for help. Word from them is garbled and newsmen around President Taft think that many of the men have been killed. Soon exaggerated stories of an Indian uprising and a plot to kill the President create headlines across the country.

Coop returns to the hunt for Willie, and soon finds Lola dead. He cannot tell whether she shot herself or was killed by Willie.

Finally, Coop confronts Willie. Both are alone and as they face each other Willie draws his gun and Coop does the same, firing first. Willie is fatally wounded. Then Coop learns that Willie's gun wasn't loaded.

Coop is suddenly overwhelmed by the needless waste of a life and the futility of Willie's run. He orders that Willie be given a chief's burial.

Although *Tell Them Willie Boy Is Here* completed principal photography before Redford began filming *Butch Cassidy*, it was released to theaters after *Downhill Racer*, creating a Redford sensation when the three films opened within months of each other late in 1969.

Redford thinks Universal kept the film on the shelf for so long because it didn't know what to make of its sparse, realistic account of a 1909 manhunt for an Indian who kills his girlfriend's father in self-defense. "They were afraid, they weren't sure what it was. A lot of distributors, unless you hit them between the eyes with a sledge hammer about what the movie is, a big label, they look the other way. They're afraid to have to use their imaginations and come up with something creative to characterize it."

With Susan Clark

With Katharine Ross

With Susan Clark

Certainly complex, the film was written and directed by Abraham Polonsky, a talented man who had been on the infamous Hollywood blacklist for 20 years. After writing *Body and Soul* in 1947 (which won an Oscar) and directing *Force of Evil* in 1948, Polonsky was accused of being a Communist by the House Un-American Activities Committee. When he refused to name names in front of the committee, he was blacklisted and unable to work under his own name. He wrote several films under pseudonyms during that period (the titles of which he won't divulge), and it wasn't until he received screen credit for writing *Madigan* in 1967 that the blacklist was broken.

Willie Boy was the personal project of Polonsky, and he had his casting firmly in mind from the beginning. "No one ever turned down the script," he says proudly. "I wanted Redford and I wanted Katharine Ross long before *The Graduate*. I asked for Robert Blake, too."

According to Redford, however, he was originally asked to play the Indian and turned *that* part down. "It was a mistake—clearly," he says. He felt Polonsky should use a real Indian. He also found the role of the sheriff far more interesting "because of his neutral position to what is going on," says Redford. "It was in the gray area that I'm rather fond of in films. He saw the good and the bad on both sides and that's the character I felt I should play."

Unfortunately, the studio didn't feel Polonsky should use real Indians. "They saw it as a chance to use their contract players," complains Redford. "I was sick and tired of seeing Indians—many of whom I had know personally and been friendly with—depicted on the screen in a way that really annoyed me. And I thought what better opportunity than this, a real Indian story, to let the Indians play themselves. But the studio saw it differently."

Redford also thought the representation of the Indians in *Willie Boy* was all wrong. "It wasn't real. Indians don't talk that much—and they don't talk like that. Polonsky was still carrying forth the liberal causes from the Thirties and he put dialogue in the mouths of Indians that didn't really fit. Indians don't talk like people out of Hell's Kitchen. They don't say, 'Your hand is white, mine is red—does that make us any different?' That kind of stuff gives you a little cringe."

But Redford, basically, liked the script. "I liked the movie. I liked what it was trying to say." And he elaborated further on why the sheriff role appealed to him:

"He's a loner who can't make the adjustment to modern society. He was raised with Indians, but around 1909, the Indians were beginning to be squelched. He has no respect for the white community, for the attitude of 'I think I'll go out and kill me a few Indians,' but he has to maintain law and order. In the process of the chase he discovers a lot about himself.

"In the beginning, he's an uncommitted man; at the end of the film you should feel he's a man committed. He learns, he grows. I was attracted by the idea of playing a simple man who grows."

Filming was done in Southern California, and Redford maintains that Polonsky's absence from the Hollywood scene created problems. "There was a whole group there, camera crew and so forth, that was waiting for him to show signs of being dated. So he took great precautions not to seem that way. One of them was to be definite. He had this big defense thing going about being in control. He was like Rommel. A lot of times he was being definite when I don't think he had a clue what he wanted to do. This created problems with the cameraman, Conrad Hall, who knows what he's doing. He was about to direct a film himself, and the toughest time to get a cameraman is just the moment when he's going to fly the coop and be a director, because he disputes everything. Abe won, I think, but let's face it, the look of the film was Conrad's."

Asked if the tensions on the set affected his performance, Redford replies quickly, "Nothing affects my performance. I don't really work within the confines of a set anyway. I don't know how to elaborate on that."

Once the film was released, it garnered high critical praise for all involved. But Polonsky was unhappy with the distribution in America, which he felt was vastly inferior to that in Europe, and blamed Universal when the film was not a huge success commercially. He also criticized Redford, who, he claimed, loved the film until associates told him the Indian is really the star of the film. "Redford's ego got in the way," Polonsky was quoted as saying, "so he's been going around saying he hates the film now."

Redford is amazed when this is related to him. "That's totally wrong. Jesus, that's incredible. In fact, it was sort of the opposite as I recall. Blake was going around on talk shows at the time, really bitter and hostile towards me, feeling he got screwed in the release of the film.

"I didn't have anything to do with the movie's release or how it was promoted. As a matter of fact, I got him the job—I fought to get him when the studio didn't want him. It was a strange gratitude on the part of Blake—but then he seemed to be fairly bitter all around."

Redford did have reservations about the film when he saw it. "But," he says, "it had nothing to do with

With Robert Blake

131

Blake or anyone stealing the picture. Again, it was the Indians. I felt they were being portrayed as whites. And I thought Polonsky—through insecurity because he hadn't made a film in so long or because of pressure from the studio—backed off from the kind of film he wanted to make. The script was terrific. I don't think the movie realized fifty percent of its potential as a script. Had Abe been left to his own devices, he probably would have made the movie I thought he was going to make."

REVIEWS

"Tell Them Willie Boy Is Here is an admirable motion picture—taut, clean, precise in scene and image, cinematically cogent. It is not quite, though, the picture it might have been, and perhaps should have been . . . The film's faults come from Polonsky's deviation from Willie's story into a half-relevant romance between the sheriff and the liberated lady Indian-agent, from his romanticizing his story, from his occasional slipping into Western cliche—and most of all from his evading an obligatory scene. Willie's girl is found dead by the posse. Polonsky refuses to tell us whether she shot herself or Willie shot her. (In life, he shot her.) And by omitting the death scene, he cops out on a major insight into Willie's character and his relationship with the girl . . . Blake and Redford give performances of really exceptional skill. Blake's Willie Boy is reticent, adamantly self-sufficient, resolute—a man to and for himself. Redford plays the sheriff as a man inextricably caught between apparent duty and real justice. Their final encounter is spare, astringent and powerful."

WINFRED BLEVINS,
Los Angeles Herald Examiner

"Abraham Polonsky's *Tell Them Willie Boy Is Here,* only the second film ever and first in twenty years for the longtime blacklistee, is perhaps the most complex and original American film since *Bonnie and Clyde.* A powerful unfoldment of a particular incident in U.S. history, the film becomes, by extension, a deeply personal and radical vision of the past and future of this country . . . Polonsky is not a director who 'works through' his actors. Thespians are simply tools of his vision—their presences, more than their abilities, are needed. Nobody's going to win any acting awards for their work herein. Still, Redford's 'presence' is magnificent, always suggesting the classically-structured, powerful-but-weak American."

BYRO,
Variety

"The novelty of *Willie Boy* lies not in the chase itself but in showing us the misery of the American Indian. Yet, as a piece of film-making, it is not exceptional—its main fault being that, while one is moved by the plight of the twentieth-century Indian, there is hardly any emotional response to Willie, the individual. We are not made to care about him as a person. Also, if the director had substituted a white man for his hero, he would simply have made one more formula Western."

CLIVE HIRSCHHORN,
London Sunday Express

With Susan Clark

"Abraham Polonsky has written and directed an extraordinary film that exists on several levels and is consequently much more complicated and profound than any plot synopsis could suggest. For those incapable of seeing beneath the surface it can still be highly enjoyed as an exciting story told for its own sake—a factor that speaks well for potential commercial success . . . *Willie Boy* moves at a marvelously controlled pace and has suspense, which is why it has so much strength merely as an 'entertainment' . . . The characters are solid and three-dimensional and brilliantly played."

Motion Picture Herald

"*Willie Boy* is a fascinating, taut, but flawed chase story, a dangerous game of 'cowboys and Indians' played from the point of view of the Indians. One of its biggest virtues is also one of its biggest flaws: the casting of that powerful actor Robert Redford as 'Cooper,' the sheriff pursuing Willie. Mr. Redford's strength and dramatic magnetism dominate any film he's in. His performance overpowers that of Robert Blake as Willie, and tips the film away from its focus."

LOUISE SWEENEY,
Christian Science Monitor

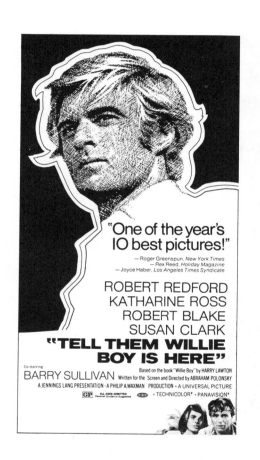

134

(Above and left) With Katharine Ross

Robert Blake and Katharine Ross

LITTLE FAUSS AND BIG HALSY

A Paramount Release (1970). In Panavision and
Movielab Color. 99 minutes. Rated R.

CAST

Big Halsy, Robert Redford; *Little Fauss,* Michael J.
Pollard; *Rita Nebraska,* Lauren Hutton; *Seally Fauss,*
Noah Beery; *Mom Fauss,* Lucille Benson; *Moneth,*
Linda Gaye Scott; *Photographer,* Ray Ballard; *Marcy,*
Shara St. John; *Rick Nifty,* Ben Archibek.

CREDITS

Produced by Albert J. Ruddy; *Directed by* Sidney J.
Furie; *Written by* Charles Eastman; *Photography by*
Ralph Woolsey, A.S.C.; *Production Manager:* Terry
Morse; *Art Direction by* Larry Paull; *Assistant Director:* Terry Morse; *Edited by* Argyle Nelson, Jr.

Michael Pollard, Lauren Hutton and Redford on location

SYNOPSIS

At a small-time motorcycle track in Arizona, an inept Little Fauss trails the field. His most loyal boosters are his parents—Seally, who has the sanitary concession, and Mom, who runs the catering truck. Mom tries to interest a photographer in taking Little's picture, but he has his lens trained on the long scar on the back of Halsy Knox, a lithe, swaggering hustler who feeds his girl the remains of a sandwich he stole from Mom.

At the end of the race, Little brings his wrecked bike to the Fauss trailer truck. Halsy asks for a push to start his old pick-up truck, but doesn't offer to help the Fausses load their equipment. Seally, muttering he won't help undesirable cyclists, leaves Halsy stranded. Halsy gets help from the photographer, who spends the night in a motel with Halsy and his girl. At dawn Halsy extricates himself from the other two, takes the photographer's camera and wallet, and slips away.

In the next town, Halsy stops at a cycle shop for parts. The mechanic turns out to be Little, who is won over by Halsy's smooth talk and repairs the bike without charge. They become friends and Little invites Halsy to be his guest for the weekend. The two enter an amateur event and Little breaks his leg in a fall caused by Halsy's reckless riding. After winning the race, Halsy takes his time returning to Little, but eventually does, with a new girlfriend.

Halsy convinces Little to join him in some new plans. Since he's suspended, from racing, Halsy will enter pro races in California, where he's not known, using Little's name, license and bike, and they'll split the winnings. Little goes along as the mechanic, after leaving home without his parents' blessing. Halsy celebrates a second-place finish in the next race with two admiring girls. Later, he confides to Little that he can't get any truly decent girls.

The start of the next race is delayed when a naked girl, Rita Nebraska, stumbles toward the track. Abandoned by a group of hoodlum cyclists, she enters Halsy's truck. He wants to throw her out, but Little's kindness prevails. After the race, Rita, wearing their clothes, joins them as a passenger. Halsy favors leaving Rita but Little insists he wants a girl of his own, so Rita stays on.

After drinking too much at a roadhouse, Little and Halsy have an argument over Rita. The partnership is broken. Halsy drives off with Rita, whom he now regards as his girl friend, and Little goes home, his loneliness soon increased by the death of his father.

Just as Little is training for a return to racing, Halsy shows up at the Fauss home with a pregnant Rita. Halsy wants Little to ride sidehack with him. He also tries to leave Rita with Little. An unforgiving Little says he'll ride solo at Sears Point and rejects the

With Lauren Hutton

With Michael Pollard

idea of caring for Rita and her baby.

Little wins first place at a small track while Halsy and another partner win at another California track. Rita has her baby after being rushed to the hospital by the track ambulance.

Some months later, Little tells Halsy he's about to be drafted, and Halsy tells him to crash his bike and be reclassified. Before long, Rita leaves Halsy. Then Halsy brags to Little about all the racing and sponsorship offers he's turned down. Little knows there have been no offers. They drive their bikes to Sears Point and are among the hundred bikers to speed around the track. They are lost in the crowd. They

will always be among those who make no significant mark nor leave a permanent trace.

"Little Fauss and Big Halsy," says Sidney Furie, the man who directed it, "was written by Charles Eastman. He very much wanted to direct it himself. They should have let him."

Furie had misgivings about the project from the beginning. Once producer Albert Ruddy decided that Eastman shouldn't direct it and Furie should, he gave the script to Furie and made it clear he didn't want any changes made. "I read it," Furie says, "and said, 'It's

With Shara St. John

With Michael Pollard

With Lauren Hutton

got the best dialogue I ever read and it's got some wonderful scenes but we've got a problem with the ending.' But for some strange reason that happens to people I got talked out of my feelings. I started the picture and talked myself into thinking it was going to work."

Furie didn't have any reservations about the lead actors. He thought Redford was perfect to play Big Halsy, a handsome, swaggering, womanizing, thieving charmer who races motorcycles and uses people for his own ends. And Michael J. Pollard was practically born to play Little Fauss, a funny-looking, unsure, shy "second stringer" who idolized Halsy.

Halsy was a character Redford was anxious to play. "It was a very different role from what I'd been doing. He's very verbose for a next to illiterate type of guy. He's a rake, an absolute cad, scroungy and raunchy. There was nothing subtle in that role. It was fun to go that way for a shot." Redford also liked the milieu of the film. A "bike nut," he felt a certain kinship to Halsy. "It was the way I grew up in Van Nuys, with motorcycles and hot rods. You could say my love of motorcycles has something to do with sexual drive, but if you try to analyze why you like things you take the sense of fun out of them."

Furie thinks Redford definitely understood Halsy. "He felt for this guy. I think he had it in the back of his mind that had it not been for taking the right path in his youth he might easily have been one of these guys."

The first time Furie met Redford, at a story conference, he found him "unlike any other actor I'd ever met. If you didn't know he was an actor because you recognized him you'd think he was a young executive. He's personable, matter of fact, no bullshit, no small-talk, no talking about girls or drinking or what he did last night."

Furie found the same matter-of-fact Redford attitude during the filming in San Francisco, Los Angeles, Phoenix, and quite a few smaller towns. The production operated like a traveling road company, filming in a different town every few days. The motorcycle racing sequences were filmed at the Willow Springs Raceway, 100 miles from L.A., the Manzanita Speedway in Phoenix and at Sears Point during the first national championship road races there.

The filming went fairly smoothly, with a few exceptions. Redford and Pollard didn't get along very well. "They're completely different," says Furie. "It wasn't that there was friction between them, but they were hardly friendly. And I'm not going to say Pollard was stoned most of the time, but he was. He only missed a half day because of it, but it certainly made it hard for him to relate to Redford in any way other than as his character."

Once, Furie and Redford had an angry exchange.

"We were doing a scene and trying to line up a long lens shot," Furie explains, "and Redford kept moving and we couldn't line it up. So I said, 'Listen, I'm having trouble,' and he said 'Too bad.' So I stopped and said, 'Come here, I want to talk to you. You're right, it is too bad. Because if you ever do that again, I'm leaving. I don't need to stay and hear that and be embarrassed in front of people. I'm trying to make this picture. If you don't think the shot's a good idea, let's talk about it. But if you do, don't tell me, "Too bad." I don't treat you that way.'

"I don't think he meant it quite the way it sounded, but he respected that I put my feelings on the line and didn't harbor it. After that, he was very sensitive to my feelings."

The reason for this atypical behavior on the part of Redford, who is usually easy to work with and highly courteous, is clear when Redford talks about *Little Fauss*. "I was so involved in *Downhill Racer* when I made *Little Fauss and Big Halsy*, it was like doing something in your sleep almost. I didn't shortcut the performance; I mean, I gave, but I have very little memory of the experience. And I was also very detached on that picture. I didn't have any hostilities or anything so much; it's just that I was so preoccupied with these other things. And I was also beat."

Furie has very little memory of *Little Fauss and Big Halsy* as well. "You tend to put out of your mind efforts that aren't successful. For me, the film was very unsatisfying. I was kidding myself that it would work with the ending the way it was in the script. And it wasn't just a matter of adding an ending, that's something you have to plant the seeds of in the beginning. Eastman wouldn't work with us because he couldn't direct it, and Ruddy wouldn't let me work on the script. So I was just showing up and telling people where to stand, I wasn't in on the *storytelling*, and the director should always be in on that."

"That was Furie's fault," says Redford. "Everyone told him all the way through—he should have shot the ending the author wrote. The original ending was a good one. That was the best screenplay of any film I've ever done, in my opinion. It was without doubt the most interesting, the funniest, the saddest, the most real—and original. Furie just never understood it—he kept making cartoons out of it. He didn't shoot the ending that was written because he didn't understand what the movie was about.

"And he had a big ego problem—he didn't want to listen to suggestions. Things were dealt with in a large, splashy, cartoon way rather than in the sensitive, finely tuned way of the script. There was a terrific ear that went into writing that script and it was a bad ear that went into making it. The author was done a disservice. Furie really can't blame anyone but himself for the way the picture turned out—it was his interpretation. He made it."

But both Redford and Furie believe the film "has some wonderful scenes." And Furie thinks it contains "some of the best acting Redford has ever done."

Many critics agreed with Furie's assessment. The film received mostly negative reviews, but Redford's performance was praised. Furie feels the quality of the Redford acting was lost because the film was commercially unsuccessful. "When something's a big hit, everybody says, 'Yeah, he was great in that.' But, if it isn't, you never hear anyone say, 'You know, Redford did some of his best acting in *Little Fauss and Big Halsy.*' That isn't the way it is in this business.

"But Redford's acting is superb in this. He's completely different than he was in *Butch,* or *The Sting* or *Downhill Racer.* People criticize him saying he's always Redford. Well, he isn't. He might always look Redford, but he really does become the character he's playing."

Furie pauses thoughtfully and says, "You know, there's a certain unreality about acting. But Redford's the realest actor I've ever met. He's just a guy who happens to be an actor. It's his work, and that's where it starts and ends. After we finished *Little Fauss,* Redford let me use his house at Sundance, and that taught me more about him than I had learned during all of the filming. There was nothing pretentious or phony about the place. It was easy living—the place he escapes to."

Little Fauss and Big Halsy opened in New York on October 21, 1970. The next day, Lola Redford gave birth to her third child, a girl, Amy Hart.

REVIEWS

"*Little Fauss and Big Halsy* embodies a number of the going trends in the film business. It is, in the shallowest sense, a bike picture trailing in the fumes of the lucrative *Easy Rider.* At the same time, it is a 'road picture,' whose itinerant narrative allows the camera to take in huge and beautiful chunks of the American landscape. And its theme is the familiar personal search, the protagonist racing down the road in quest of himself.

"But for all this surface trendiness, *Fauss and Halsy* uses its conventions, not for their own sake, but as a way of examining the values of American life. And it explores these values the hard way—by getting beneath the skin of its protagonist. Robert Redford plays Halsy, and if you want to label this movie, then call it a Redford movie. For Halsy is independent, lonely, running, remote, obsessed—all the qualities we have come to expect from a Redford hero.

"Redford realizes Halsy through small gestures; his eyes never still, always searching out some advantage; his smile the counterfeit amiability of the used-car salesman; his speech the quick, slick cadences of the

The bumbling burglars: Ron Liebman, George Segal, Redford and Paul Sand

Eyeing the Hot Rock

SYNOPSIS

Just released from prison, John Archibald Dortmunder enters into a scheme with his brother-in-law Andrew Kelp to steal a priceless diamond belonging to an African nation. The diamond is on display at the Brooklyn Museum. The two make a deal with Dr. Amusa, an ambassador of a rival African nation which wants the stone at any cost.

Enlisting the help of Murch and Alan Greenberg, Dortmunder plans a meticulous burglary. Things don't go too well and Alan, caught in the glass box holding the stone, swallows the gem as he is captured.

After conferring with Alan's father, a devious and greedy lawyer named Abe, the four break into jail and rescue Alan. But he tells them he doesn't have the diamond: he hid it in the police precinct where he was first brought after his arrest. Dressed in police uniforms, they break into the station house by setting off a series of bombs. But they can't find the gem where Alan says he hid it, and soon realize that Abe has gotten to it first, and put it in his safe deposit box.

For the fourth time, Dortmunder tries to get the hot rock. He hypnotizes a bank clerk and finally takes possession of the prize. As he leaves the bank, he sees Abe and Dr. Amusa rush in. But he has won. The Hot Rock is his.

After four films which required a great deal from Redford, either in terms of characterization or filming exigencies, *The Hot Rock* was a welcome relief. A lighthearted caper film, it was shot on location entirely in New York in just three months, and it had no message—its only *raison d' être* was to bring enjoyment to its audience.

For these reasons, Redford was as anxious to do the film as he had been the far more meaningful *Willie Boy* and *Downhill Racer*. "I always wanted to do a caper film just for the fun of it." he says. "And I wanted to work with an ensemble group of good actors. I like George Segal and Paul Sand and Ron Leibman, and all the other actors involved were strong actors and I was enthusiastic about that."

There was another, more pressing reason why Redford decided to do the film. "I needed the money. I was flat broke—really had financial problems at the time. It's the only film I've ever done with money as a principal consideration."

The film re-united Redford and William Goldman, who had won an Oscar for his *Butch Cassidy* screenplay. Based on a novel by Donald Westlake, Goldman had originally written his script with George Segal in mind for the part Redford eventually played and George C. Scott in mind for the Segal role. It seems that most writers' casting ideas are rarely completely realized.

Hired to direct the film was English director Peter

Yates, whose *Bullitt* had been praised as *the* chase film of the '60s. When *The Hot Rock* opened to tepid reviews, many critics cited Yates' direction as the main problem, and Redford tends to agree with this assessment.

"Yates was essentially an action director," says Redford, "and being English, he had an English humor. *The Hot Rock* was a very American movie, with a very American humor about it. Yates was in the process of being Americanized, but the movie suffered because he really didn't understand American humor."

There are some wonderful moments in *The Hot Rock,* and the film is easy enough to take as entertainment. "It's certainly not the most substantive piece of work I've done," says Redford. "But I don't regret it. I don't regret anything I've done. If I had my life to live over, I'd do exactly the same things. I'd turn down *Love Story* again, and *The Godfather* and *French Connection* and *Virginia Woolf*—those just weren't things that interested me at the time. And the ones I did, I'll stand by—even though they may not have turned out quite right."

149

REVIEWS

"The virtues of *The Hot Rock* are nearly all negative. It is a crime picture—comic caper subdivision—that is full of action but happily free of the ugly violence that has marred such recent popular successes as *Dirty Harry*. It is also innocent of the attempt to make jokes about kinky sex that made *$*—a more direct competitor—so distasteful. In short, it's a chaste chase. Unfortunately, there's not much more to say in its favor . . . Being wrapped up in a package is evidently not the same as being wrapped up in your work. It's hard to say exactly what went wrong, but maybe all hands thought that a project that looked so good on paper didn't require their full creative energies. Or maybe it's impossible to mobilize those energies for just another venture into a genre that was overworked before they even began . . . As for Redford and Segal, they present themselves with consumer-approved charm, but not much more."

RICHARD SHICKEL,
Life

"*The Hot Rock* . . . is the first fun picture of the new year. In the 11 months ahead it's going to be hard to beat the tricks and suspense perpetrated by director Peter Yates and scripter William Goldman and daringly and dangerously executed by a perfect cast . . . Redford and Segal complement each other as did Redford and Paul Newman in *Butch Cassidy* . . . Redford's great scene shows him alone, leisurely working his way through a bank into the safety deposit vault, retrieving the stone before Mostel gets there and getting away without being detected. It's a joy to watch."

WANDA HALE,
New York Daily News

"Redford's supercool pose of *Butch Cassidy and the Sundance Kid* and *Downhill Racer* has sunk to the inexpressiveness of catatonia in *The Hot Rock*. The director obviously has only a rudimentary feeling for comic timing. There are gaps wide enough for you to stretch out and fall asleep in. I have to say in fairness that *Hot Rock* is good wholesome fun for adolescents. My son and a classmate enjoyed it immensely. And, though less enthusiastic myself, I did like the action sections, the gum-snapping bravado of getaway driver Ron Leibman and Zero Mostel's bellowing shyster lawyer."

JOSEPH GELMIS,
Newsday

Dortmunder and Kelp discuss arrangements of the heist with Dr. Amusa. (With George Segal and Moses Gunn)

"The script for *The Hot Rock* has more holes than a sieve and is so ludicrous in places that vast pieces of coherence seem to be missing. But Peter Yates' direction is crisp and stylish, and the witty ensemble playing of Robert Redford, George Segal, Ron Leibman and Paul Sand, as the clumsy thieves, looks like the Mighty Carson Art Players doing a takeoff on *Rififi*. Highly dispensable fluff, but if you've already seen Richard Brooks' brilliant *$*, a vastly superior caper film in every conceivable way, *The Hot Rock* is a harmless enough way to kill a couple of hours. Or you could always wait for it to show up next year on television."

REX REED

"In the leading roles, the casting is four-fifths pure inspiration—and perhaps it's that fifth that's the bothersome element. Robert Redford is the fifth that is first, the mastermind of the gang, the perfect-crime planner who spends too much time in prison, a patsy for his scheming brother-in-law despite being the brains and the ultimate technician, whose frustrations are such that he winds up munching Gelusil tablets on the job. And Redford is just a little too all-American handsome, a bit too sophisticated and "star quality" for the company he keeps in this film. He is actor enough to carry off the role—but in context it seems more role than realism."

JUDITH CRIST,
New York

Abe Greenburg gives the guys the plans to the prison his son is in so they can spring him. (With Zero Mostel)

Breaking into the jail (with George Segal and Paul Sand)

"The cast and the plot are both promising, but it just doesn't come off. Segal and Leibman mug as though they were playing vaudeville; Sand underplays until he is hardly noticeable; Mostel operates at half speed in a ludicrous Southern colonel costume that is out of phase with the rest of the film, and only Redford comes through with the right kind of smoothness and control."

GAIL ROCK,
Women's Wear Daily

"Redford, as always, is the center of attention. You can't take your eyes off him; you keep thinking he could do anything, yet somehow he never does. From film to film, he carries this aura of betrayed promise, something sad and inaccessible which should be drawn on as the stuff of characterization instead of hovering like a mist around the edges."

MOLLY HASKELL,
Village Voice

"Direction of the four hoods is efficient if not fully successful because of script factors. Redford continues to reveal a compelling screen presence even if only about fifty percent of his potential ever seems to be utilized . . ."

MURF.,
Variety

Redford, Segal and director Peter Yates map out a scene

He also gave Michael Ritchie a call and told him he wanted to do a political film. Ritchie said, "Great. Do you have a book?"

"No," Redford replied.

"Do you have a story idea?"

"No."

"Well, do you have a writer?"

"Not exactly."

Still, Ritchie thought it was a pretty good concept and agreed to work with Redford on the project. They got together and batted around the idea. The picture they wanted to do would take a young, idealistic, "clean" lawyer who enters politics as an alternative to the system and who winds up just like the phony politicians he detested.

Redford and Ritchie decided to hire Jeremy Larner, who had been a speech writer for Eugene McCarthy and knew the workings of the grass-roots campaign their movie candidate, Bill McKay, was running. "I had worked in the Tunney campaign, which was in many ways similar to what he wanted to portray," says Ritchie, "so we had a lot of good background anecdotes to throw into the picture."

Despite reports which said that they had a particular candidate in mind (Bobby Kennedy was mentioned the most) Ritchie denies this. "We really didn't think in terms of the Kennedys. They were interested in politics from the beginning. If we had anyone at all in mind, it was someone like Ralph Nader or Jerry Brown, the kind of guy who hates politics, thinks it's all bullshit, then gets involved in it. What happens to him? That's what we wanted to show."

After developing a script, Redford attempted to get studio backing for his project. If *The Candidate* was similar to *Downhill Racer* in terms of its theme of winning and losing and its loner protagonist, as well as the men involved with it (Ritchie and Redford), it was similar too in the difficulty Redford had in selling the idea to a studio. "The political film is poison at the box-office" was the conventional wisdom Redford was up against. As he puts it, "I was put in the lousy position of taking the idea around and acting it out on the rug, just like with *Downhill Racer*."

Redford remembers wryly that Stanley Jaffe, then president of Paramount, nearly fell asleep during one

of his "rug performances." "They kept giving me the pink slip routine—you know, the one where they say 'You're a nice guy but. . .'."

After several other executives admitted they were afraid of anything political, Redford finally got an O.K. from Dick Zanuck, his nemesis at the start of *Butch Cassidy,* who had lost a power struggle at 20th Century-Fox and moved to Warner Bros. Zanuck told Redford to go ahead and make his movie as he saw fit.

Redford told Ritchie that he wanted to make the movie in New York, where he was familiar with the political process. Ritchie convinced him that California was the one spot where a candidacy like Bill McKay's would be taken seriously, and filming began near Los Angeles on November 29, 1971. The shooting schedule was tight—the film had to be ready for release by June of 1972, in time for the presidential election.

Making the film wasn't a pleasant experience for Redford. "It wasn't easy for me to play the role," says Redford. "I don't like crowds, groups. I don't like wearing a suit. I'm apolitical, which is why the picture is essentially apolitical."

Even more than that, filming *The Candidate* confirmed Redford's worst suspicions about the political process in America. One of the filming ploys of the crew was to set up whistle stops for Redford and present him to crowds as a real candidate for office. Redford would make speeches which said nothing, and he was amazed that he held people's attention. "They were buying what I was saying. And I'm sure a lot of them were prepared to vote for me too."

The feeling of what it's like to be a real candidate also caused Redford some disquiet. "When they were ready to film the scene about the ticker-tape parade on Montgomery Street in San Francisco," he says, "I wanted to be skiing in Utah. I'd had only four days off in the whole film, and I was mad that I had to come back for that scene. I resented it. I was down. Anyway, the scene was set up by an actual advance man who went around arranging for all the secretaries in the area to tear off their calendar pages and throw them out their windows at noon. And when I was in that car, with all those people who thought I was a real candidate reaching for me, and all those thousands of calendar pages coming down—well, in five seconds I was on a 'high.' You feel you could go for days without eating or sleeping, and at that time you would believe anything good about yourself. It's like finding a piece of kryptonite, you feel so powerful."

Because the script was constantly being re-worked, the filming of *The Candidate* was an evolutionary process. Many of the ideas and scenes were filmed, discarded, picked up again. "Redford had the ideas for the beginning and the end," says Ritchie, "and I got the ideas for the scene where he breaks up in the TV

After being introduced to Natalie Wood at a fundraising event, McKay asks an aid, "Who *is* she?"

The candidate and his campaign manager. (With Peter Boyle)

McKay mulls it over

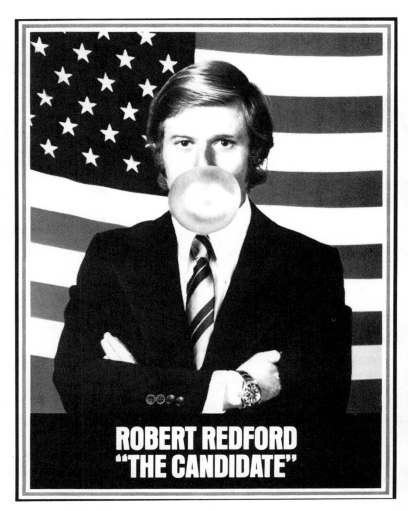

**ROBERT REDFORD
"THE CANDIDATE"**

McKay meets the people

McKay and Jarmon both show up at the Malibu fire. (With Don Porter)

Father congratulates son on his victory (with Melvyn Douglas)

McKay and Jarmon on TV: The Great Debate

161

studio and the Malibu fire thing from working in the Tunney campaign. Most of the fine shadings of the McKay character came from Larner—thinks like his vanity getting the better of him without his realizing it, and the relationship with his father."

Ritchie says the scene in the car, when McKay mocks his upcoming speech by turning it into gobbledygook, was nearly not filmed. "It didn't read that well on paper, and we weren't sure it would work, so we kept putting it off. Finally we were finished with everything else, and Larner said, 'Let's forget about it, it probably won't work anyway.' But Bob and I wanted to try it, so we filmed it. And, of course, it turned out to be probably the key scene in the whole picture."

Another scene was filmed, and never appeared in the finished movie. "It was a bit about how McKay, angered that he's been upstaged by his opponent at the Malibu fire, goes swimming in his hotel pool and vigorously works off his anger. While he's swimming, a sixteen-year-old girl slips out of a robe and into the pool, nude, and swims over to him. She says, 'Aren't you from Van Nuys?' and he says 'Yes.' She says, 'Do you know Pinky King?' He says, 'No.' 'Oh, I thought you'd know Pinky King.' Well, we showed it to a preview audience and nobody laughed, nobody understood it. We were trying to show the lengths to which political groupies will go to get close to a candidate, but it just didn't work.

"It did give us probably the funniest thing that happened during the filming, though. The day we shot it, it was forty-one degrees out and a fierce wind was blowing. Redford had the flu and a one-hundred-two degree fever. No one wanted him to do it, but he insisted. He gets into the pool, shivering, and everyone figures he'll come out with double pneumonia. Meanwhile, the girl is nervous as hell because she's never done a nude scene before and I'm telling her, 'It's O.K., this is dignified, people do nude scenes all the time, the crew won't leer.' She has to get drunk on Manischewitz before she can do it, but finally she gets into the pool and we start shooting. Suddenly out of the bushes jump Peter Boyle and five other cast members, male and female, stark naked, and they dive bomb the pool. And just as fast as they got in they streak back to their rooms. The assistant director is yelling, 'What happened to the security around here?' and we're all hysterical. But I don't think the girl appreciated it very much."

Another improvised scene was one in which Natalie Wood visits a campaign rally of McKay's. Unfortunately, he doesn't know who she is. The scene is one of the rare occasions on film when two good friends share an inside joke with the public.

Once it came time to share *The Candidate* with the public, in July of 1972, it was hailed as a virtual masterpiece. Critics praised the film's realism, its hard-hitting look at the seamy, dehumanizing side of politics. The film was considered so unsparing in its depiction of the political process, in fact, that it created a controversy when public officials like Bella Abzug of New York criticized it as presenting an unfair picture. "What worries me," said Abzug, "is that young people who get disillusioned as quickly as Larner will find their worst fears confirmed by this simplistic film, and see politics as a determinist process that moves its participants from compromises into double-talk and sell-outs. There's still room for men and women with passion and principles in our society. They just need staying power and more confidence in the electorate than *The Candidate* is willing to concede."

However true Ms. Abzug's opinion might have been, the course of American history in the two years after the release of *The Candidate* proved it to be tepid in its indictment. The Redford/Ritchie vision of corruption in American politics pales in comparison to the Watergate scandal. *That* subject would concern Redford later.

Redford's performance as McKay was itself so realistic and compelling that many critics went so far as to suggest seriously he consider running for office. "I've thought about it," he says. "I've thought about how I wouldn't like it. I can't imagine any politician surviving the campaign process and remaining totally his own man. I think a politician has to sell a little piece of himself, and I don't want to."

REVIEWS

"Political themes have never been any more successful on the screen than, say, movies about the American Revolution. *The Candidate* blows that old taboo sky high. Not only is it the most interesting and entertaining movie I've ever seen about American politics, but it also achieves the provocative distinction of probably getting Robert Redford a nomination for President. I have seldom seen a performer so firmly entrenched in the nuances of a role; even when the film is not being improvised into moments of throbbing realism, it soars with the sweat and sweetness of total naturalism in scenes that never seem rehearsed ... *The Candidate* is like a string of Fourth of July firecrackers, exploding in joy, confusion and exhausting brilliance. Coming, as it does, in a fitful election year, it smacks of commercial motivation, but it is so clever, riveting and honest that I, for one, am willing to forgive all transgressions. Its relevance and entertainment value far outweigh its opportunism. *The Candidate* certainly gets my vote."

REX REED

"*The Candidate* is perhaps the most honest film about American politics ever made. In the title role, Robert Redford commands a formidable range of expression and his character undergoes subtle, nefarious change. In some human way, he manages to remain likeable . . . Director Ritchie uses his eye for detail to best advantage during the conventions, TV debates and on election night. Much groundwork is laid at the outset and the film slows toward the middle, but the pace seems to support the repetitive nature as well as the impending drama of the campaign."

Show

"Beautifully photographed, exquisitely acted, subtly directed, *The Candidate* is not a boffo, wham-bang movie that approaches you head-on and smashes you in the face. Rather it tails you down the street, sidles up to you at the crossing, whispers its message and then leaves you with a wow on your lips right in the middle of traffic . . . Robert Redford, the king of cool, has come up with the coolest political film ever."

ART UNGER

"There is a distinctive distant cool perspective that adds something of special value to the film. Though the ending does give *The Candidate* something of a fairy tale flavor in which the good guys triumph, there is enough realistic portrayal of people and motives to inspire most Americans to a few moments of sincere introspection. What's also awfully good about *The Candidate* is the fact that Redford makes a politician most of us would be happy to vote for. When was the last time we had one sounding like that? Bobby?"

ARCHER WINSTEN,
New York Post

"*The Candidate* has no script to speak of. The characters are not fully drawn. But these weaknesses matter very little. For here at long last is a film that shows, with cutting detail, what a dirty business politics really is. Done in an almost journalistic style, it details one man's campaign with such deadly accuracy that one arrives at an intimate understanding of just how political kingmakers play America's No. 1 con game—Politics. Robert Redford is perfectly cast as the dream candidate. He's got everything; the Kennedy looks, a boyish sincerity and yes, even charisma. In fact Redford looks so good on the campaign trail the Democrats, in the unlikely case of a convention deadlock, might consider him a viable candidate for President. He's a sure winner."

KATHLEEN CARROLL,
New York Daily News

"Redford is superb as McKay—ideal poster fodder. A natural, shirt-sleeves rolled, grin flashing to go up against the silverlined, sleek satisfactions of his Republican opponent, Redford displays too the inner man, keeps the heart and soul visible beneath the weary antics and growing cynicism. He understands not just the glib and easy but the voids in the man, the fuzzy edges of emotion that McKay himself cannot pencil in."

BRIDGET BYRNE,
Los Angeles Herald Examiner

163

Jeremiah gets ready to take to the mountains

JEREMIAH JOHNSON

A Warner Bros. Release (1972). In Panavision and Technicolor. 108 minutes. Rated **PG**.

CAST

Jeremiah Johnson, Robert Redford; *Bear Claw*, Will Geer; *Del Gue*, Stefan Gierasch; *Crazy Woman*, Allyn Ann McLerie; *Robidoux*, Charles Tyner; *Swan*, Delle Bolton; *Caleb*, Josh Albee; *Paints His Shirt Red*, Joaquin Martinez; *Reverend*, Paul Benedict; *Qualen*, Matt Clark; *Lebeaux*, Richard Angarola; *Lieut. Mulvey*, Jack Colvin.

CREDITS

Produced by Joe Wizan; *Directed by* Sydney Pollack; *Screenplay by* John Milius and Edward Anhalt; *Based on the novel* Mountain Man *by* Vardis Fisher *and the story* "Crow Killer" *by* Raymond W. Thorp and Robert Bunker; *Photography by* Duke Callaghan; *Art Direction by* Ted Haworth; *Edited by* Thomas Stanford; *Music by* John Rubenstein and Tim McIntire; *Assistant Director:* Mike Moder.

Jeremiah Johnson, mountain man

SYNOPSIS

Sick of civilization, Jeremiah Johnson decides to become a mountain man. His first winter proves almost fatal because of his inexperience in coping with the harsh elements. Fortunately, he meets another mountain man, Bear Claw, seasoned to the ways of the wild. Bear Claw takes Johnson in and shares his knowledge with him. Johnson's next winter is more successful as he puts into practice Bear Claw's advice.

Johnson's solitude is broken one day when he happens upon an Indian massacre of a settler's family.

The only survivors are the wife and one son. Johnson buries the dead and the woman, crazed with grief, thrusts the boy at Jeremiah and runs away. The boy is mute with shock. Johnson names him Caleb.

The next day they happen upon a bald man buried to his neck in sand by Blackfeet Indians. He has shaved his head to avoid being scalped. Johnson feels the Indians are the same ones who murdered the settler's family, and he agrees to help retrieve the man's stolen furs and horses. Finding the Indians asleep,

165

Johnson tries to take the possessions without waking them, but he fails, and a fight follows. The Indians are killed and the bald man scalps them.

Meeting up with peaceloving Flathead Indians, who are impressed by Johnson's scalps, Jeremiah is taken to their Chief, to whom he gives the horses and scalps. By Indian custom, the chief must now give a better gift or be insulted. Unenthusiastically, Johnson accepts the Chief's virgin daughter Swan. As he, Swan and Caleb leave, Johnson turns to his two companions and says, "Just don't bother me!"

The relationship between Johnson and his new wife is strained. He is brusque, she fears him, and they are unable to communicate. But before long a warmth develops. They build a cabin to make their home. Soon, a cavalry troop arrives and asks Johnson to lead it to some settlers. Johnson agrees, but when they arrive at a sacred Indian burial ground, he tells the cavalry they will have to take a 30-mile detour around it. The cavalrymen refuse and Johnson, against his judgment, goes through the grounds.

Returning home, he finds Swan and Caleb slaughtered in retaliation for his violation of the sacred ground. Half-crazed with grief, he searches for revenge and is successful in killing off Crow Indians, whose habit is to attack one by one. A legend grows about his killing prowess, and the Crows dub him Killer of Crows. His life becomes a constant battle with the Indians.

One day he visits Caleb's mother and finds her buried beside a grave the Indians have reserved for him. On it is a painting of him battling Indians. Superstition says the painting means he is already dead—or will never die.

Leaving the scene, he spots a lone Indian in the distance. After several tense minutes, the Indian salutes him. Johnson returns the salute in a gesture which is a combination of respect, fear, frustration and hatred.

Although Sydney Pollack and Redford were close friends after the filming of *This Property Is Condemned,* they couldn't agree on another project to collaborate on. Redford had talked to Pollack about directing *Downhill Racer,* but Pollack wasn't enthusiastic about it; Pollack wanted Redford for his *Castle Keep,* but Redford demurred. It wasn't until 1971 that they thought they might get together. "Bob had a script called *Liver Eatin' Johnson,"* says Pollack, and he said to me, 'I don't think it's your kind of thing, because it's kind of a bawdy comedy about a guy who eats livers, but you ought to take a look at it.' And I said, 'It sounds pretty shitty.' But I read it and laughed for the first fifty pages—one of the best beginnings I ever read. Then when this guy starts eating all those livers, I just got really turned off."

Trying to survive in the wilderness

But Pollack saw an epic, larger-than-life character in the story of a mountain man who wages a bitter struggle against the elements and Indians in order to lead a life of solitude. He and Redford decided to do it, although they agreed the script needed a great deal of work.

Warner Bros., behind the project from the start, gave Redford an advance of $200,000 upon his signing for the picture. It was money he badly needed. "Bob was in trouble in his career on legal grounds," says Pollack. "He wasn't making a lot of money from his pictures because part of them were being done as court settlements. Sundance was eating up every nickel that he had. He was broke."

The advance paid Redford was soon to complicate things badly. Warner Bros., after estimating the budget on *Jeremiah Johnson*, panicked. It was far higher than they were prepared to spend, and they informed Pollack and Redford that the film would have to be shot on the back lot, rather than on location. "Neither of us wanted to make the picture on the back lot," says Pollack. "We were in a terrible jam. And what ensued was a real testing of our friendship."

Warner Bros. offered Pollack an out, telling him they'd pay him a certain amount if he would abandon the project. "So I called Bob and said, 'If we don't want to make it on the back lot, let's don't make it.' Well, he couldn't give them back the $200,000. He was stuck. So I said to him, 'Well, wait a minute now, you're stuck but I'm not stuck.' At which point he said, 'You son of a bitch—if you walk away from this picture—I wouldn't do this to you—we went into this together!' I mean, he was really furious. So I said, 'Hey, O.K., forget it.' Bob was right.

"My agent was screaming at me, 'You can't commit suicide because he needs the $200,000. You can't make this picture on the back lot!' So I went everywhere looking for a location we could use cheap. Finally Warners let us make it if I would personally guarantee that I could film the movie in Utah for the amount of money it would have cost on the back lot."

So Pollack and Redford began filming a picture that had no script to speak of and a vastly limiting budget. There were none of the star trappings one usually associates with movie-making. "Bob had no dressing room," says Pollack. "We didn't have a john half the time. We made up the wardrobe—we just took things and tore them up and used them. We couldn't afford a wardrobe designer."

Filming in the snow-covered vastness of the Utah mountains, the production crew was not having an easy time of it. "We were so depressed," Pollack says. "We were convinced we had a disaster because we didn't know where to turn or what to do. It was in the middle of the snow and the weather was wrong every day. We'd get up, it would have snowed. You can't walk horses in the snow. They start to sink and they panic and then they start to step on you. So we had to quick go to Sears Roebuck and buy a thousand yards of chain link fence and lay it down in the snow and then put a white thing on top of that so you couldn't see the chain link fence and then go away and wait for it to snow just enough so the horse could walk on it. And it was murderous moving an arc light around. Whenever we had to do a retake, we had to get all the footprints off the snow from the first take . . . we were going crazy."

Far worse than the adverse conditions was the fact that neither Redford nor Pollack had any hard ideas about where the movie was going. They didn't feel they had a strong enough reason for the Indian massacre of Johnson's family which changes him into the legendary "Crow killer." The legend has it that the attack was a arbitrary act of carnage by the Indians, but Pollack didn't think he could make that work cinematically. He and Redford agonized night after night over how they could justify the Indians' attack and thereby give the picture a continuity and meaningfulness.

They would meet evenings in Bob's house at Sundance, near the filming site, and try to work out the problems. "We'd build a fire," relates Pollack, "and I would cook something because I'm the cook in this odd couple relationship. We'd finish dinner, sit down in front of the fireplace with a pitcher of beer, with no lights on, just looking out over the mountains where we were filming." One conversation, as Pollack describes it, went like this:

"Goddamn, Pollack," said Redford, "I bought a new tractor today. This thing is dynamite. It trowels, it cuts and sheaths and it does this stuff on the ground!"

Pollack looked at him and said, "What are we gonna do?"

Redford looked back and replied, "We can't kill all those Indians. How can we make a picture killing all those Indians?

"I know it, I know it. But what are we going to do. I mean, we've got to get it so that when the Indians kill your family it's not their fault. You've gotta screw up, you know?"

"Well, how are we gonna do that?"

Neither had an answer at this point, and Redford's last question was met with thunderous silence. Finally Pollack muttered, "Tell me about the tractor again."

"Redford just got hysterical at that," says Pollack. "But we were really depressed. We were literally making it up as we went along and every night we'd have these story conferences and there would be long silences and Bob would groan and go, 'Ooohh.' "

Presented with a wife he doesn't want, Jeremiah attempts peaceful coexistence (with Delle Bolton)

Caleb and Jeremiah run across an indisposed Del Gue (with Josh Albee and Stefan Gierasch)

Swan and Jeremiah learning to love
each other

Jeremiah and the Crazy Woman
(with Allyn Ann McLerie)

Finally, independent of Redford, Pollack and script co-author Ed Anhalt came up with the idea of Jeremiah Johnson's violating the Indians' sacred burial ground while helping cavalry men find some lost settlers. "The whole picture took on a meaning for me then," says Pollack. "That was the little bridge I needed to make the end work."

Like so many of the characters Redford has portrayed, he felt a certain kinship with Jeremiah. "I like to think I've been in parallel situations to his," he says. "But it's only when I've been lost. Mountain climbing two years ago I got lost and I didn't think I was ever going to be able to get out."

During the filming, Redford had a few moments of the same fear. Shooting an aerial view of Johnson as a solitary figure against a field of white, Pollack, Redford and the helicopter pilot were the only members of the seventy-man crew remaining. Everyone else had quit, worn out by the stress of working in the snow at altitudes of 12,000 feet, by the time Pollack decided to photograph this one last shot. Redford relates what happened next. "Sydney and the pilot dropped me off in the snow to photograph this tiny figure disappearing across the snow field. While I was walking across the snow, the copter disappeared. I didn't know where they'd gone or if they'd come back. I wondered whether Sydney was mad at me. I finally figured out he had gone for more film."

Redford turned the wait in the snow into something bordering on a spiritual experience. "There was something wonderful about that day," he says. "While they were gone it was quite an experience. I lay back in the snow and savored the soundlessness of every moment —nothing but an occasional echo over the tip of a glacier." ✓

Until the filming of *Jeremiah Johnson* was almost completed, Pollack had no definite idea of its ending. "Pollack wanted me to freeze to death," says Redford, "but I prefered to leave Johnson's fate up to the audience's imagination by having him disappear into the mountains."

For a while, that was to be the ending. "I had lots of film of him going higher and higher into the mountains," says Pollack, "but the ending turned out to be something that came entirely from Bob."

They were filming a scene in which Johnson, having fought endless battles with Indians, comes across one at a distance. They're both on horses and watch each other intensely, each unsure of the other's intentions. In the script, Redford is supposed to yell something about respecting his foes and raise his hand in a respectful salute. "It didn't work the first time," says Pollack. "He did it one way and then said, 'Let me try it this way.' So I rolled the camera and when he did it, I got chills just watching him and I said, 'O.K., that's

it,' and that's what I ended the film on. The gesture had grief in it, it had anger, it had respect, it had sadness. Everything that had gone before. I didn't tell him how to do that. It was from within himself."

Oddly, the gesture later caused some controversy when Pauline Kael criticized it. "She said I was giving the Indians the finger," says Redford. "She misinterpreted it in a way I never thought possible. It was absolutely mind-boggling. The gesture was an ad-lib response to the frustration of the pain and confusion the character was experiencing in just *continuing*. It indicated a respect for the enemy—what Rommel and Patton might have done if they had met. The criticism was especially painful to me because of my feelings and concern for the American Indian. The remark seemed to me farfetched and personal beyond the limits of responsible criticism."

Despite Kael's objections, *Jeremiah Johnson* received critical acclaim upon its release at Christmas 1972. Warner Bros. did little to promote it and the film generated little publicity, but it got excellent reviews and has become one of Redford's biggest hits, grossing over $22 million in the U.S. and Canada alone. The film is beautiful to look at, well-acted, unique—and one of Redford's best.

It certainly is his favorite film, and upon its release Redford broke his own rules of personal privacy to promote it. He went to Cannes for its presentation there, went to opening nights in places like Pocatello, Idaho. "Bob really likes that film," says Pollack. "And, even though he's usually very critical of his own work, I think he likes himself in it, too."

"I loved *Jeremiah Johnson*," says Redford. "I loved doing it and I loved the overall film. But I don't like looking at myself on film. So if I'm stuck with myself, it's very bothersome. I'm just thrilled that people seemed to like it."

REVIEWS

"*Jeremiah Johnson* is a great galumphing Paul Bunyan of a film, a sensational, mythic Western that is at once rowdy, funny, violent, poignant and tough . . . Redford is splendid as Johnson, using the explosive energy of his talent for a demanding role that ricochets from comic to tragic . . ."

LOUISE SWEENEY,
Christian Science Monitor

"*Jeremiah Johnson* seems to be the movie that *Tell Them Willie Boy Is Here* hoped to be. It is more refined, smoother, clearer, and one of the best of Robert Redford's films . . . It's a joy to watch, because for once in a Western-style script, your intelligence is not blatantly insulted. This care, a feel for the story of

the land by the people who are telling it, reappears in scene after scene . . ."

TONY VALLETA,
The Press (New Jersey)

"Let's get it straight, Bob. Blue eyes aren't enough. Steely looks won't win any prizes in these pages. If you've got a big brother, send him out and let's see what he can do. Because, Bob, to us you'll always be the aging ingenue . . . Redford is one of those light-weight talents who go a long way on looks, on knowing when to turn up the thermostat on his clean-cut boyish California-surfer sex . . . *Jeremiah Johnson* is a marvelous outdoor adventure, notable chiefly for its Rocky Mountain scenery and its splendid supporting cast. (But) Redford is Redford. His speech patterns slip and change frequently. One moment he's talking like a Bible-trained farm boy, with full, rounded phrases. The next, he's a 20th-century slum kid with idiomatic contractions. He has that kind of inconsistency that is the mark of a man without a persona. He is saved by supporting actors and by spectacular views. It should have been a better movie, with a more charismatic star."

JOSEPH GELMIS,
Newsday

" . . . Will Geer easily manages to steal every scene he is in from Redford. And this is no easy task since the young actor has strong screen presence."

GEORGE McKINNON,
Boston Globe

"That Redford, he can do anything. One minute he's a Western gunman, the next a ski champ, the next successful politician, and here he is in *Jeremiah Johnson*, playing a 'mountain man' in the Rockies in 1840s. . . .

"Redford avoids excessive linguistics but is strong on understanding and action. In any case, he makes you believe it . . ."

ARCHER WINSTEN,
New York Post

Isn't it late in the history of movies for Redford's tall-in-the-saddle star games—the stern, blank face and the quick grin like rain in the desert? Redford must want to be an old-timey hero. His underplaying has begun to seem lazy and cautious and self-protective; he never opens himself up, as a major actor must. He's playing the star games of an earlier era, and they don't mean the same things now. His model is Coop (he used the name itself in *Tell Them Willie Boy Is Here*), and he manages that dumb look; what's missing is what Coop, the Westerner, conveyed—a quiet, unshakable belief in a code and a way of life. The Westerner stood for a basic idealism, and when he used his guns it wasn't for revenge, it was for justice. Probably young audiences can no longer relate to what the Westerner stood for, but are they supposed to like Redford because he's so sheepish and silent and straight? Hell, so was Lassie. The cool silence of the Coop archetype implied depths. There are no depths in Redford that he's willing to reveal; his cool is just modern, existential chic, and it's beginning to look sullen and stubborn rather than heroic. When Redford is in a competitive buddy-buddy co-star relationship, the cool can be a put-on, but in this fake-authentic Western setting it's cool gone dank and narcissistic. The screwed-up script, by John Milius and Edward Anhalt, is empty; it exploits the appeal of the disillusioned romantic loner trying to escape the corruption of civilization, but when Jeremiah becomes corrupt himself and starts killing Indians, he's even more romantic. In the guise of gritty realism, action films have become far more primitive, celebrating tooth-and-claw revenge in a manner that would have been unthinkable in early Westerns, or even ten years ago. When the Crows, recognizing Jeremiah's courage, end their war against him, and the chief gives him a peace sign, Jeremiah signals him back, giving him the finger. In that gesture, the moviemakers load him with guilt for what the white Americans have done to the Indians, and, at the same time, ask us to laugh at the gesture, identifying with his realism. How many different kinds of consciousness can a movie diddle with? *Jeremiah Johnson* seems to have been written by vultures."

PAULINE KAEL
The New Yorker

"Sydney Pollack and Robert Redford, triumphant in his near-silent portrayal of a quiet man in a world where survival depends on the sound and the stillness, have fashioned a poetic legend, a ballad-like epic of man and nature. Of larger-than-life characters populating a mysteriously untouched but somehow teeming wilderness who meet and part and come again, each on a private quest. Pollack's achievement is his sustenance of the mood of heroic legend; Redford's is that he becomes as large as the heroes thereof—and as eternal. Yield—and you will encounter a film of penetrating beauty, and an experience that you will inevitably assimilate."

JUDITH CRIST,
New York

THE WAY WE WERE

A Columbia Release of a Rastar Productions Presentation (1973). In Panavision and Color. 118 minutes. Rated PG.

CAST

Katie Morosky, Barbra Streisand; *Hubbell Gardiner*, Robert Redford; *J.J.*, Bradford Dillman; *Carol Ann*, Lois Chiles; *George Bissinger*, Patrick O'Neal; *Paula Reisner*, Viveca Lindfors; *Rhea Edwards*, Allyn Ann McLerie; *Brooks Carpenter*, Murray Hamilton; *Bill Verso*, Herb Edelman; *Vicki Bissinger*, Diana Ewing; *Pony Dunbar*, Sally Kirkland; *Peggy Vanderbilt*, Marcia Mae Jones; *Actor*, Don Keefer; *El Morocco captain*, George Gaynes; *Army corporal*, Eric Boles; *Ash blonde*, Barbara Peterson; *Army captain*, Roy Jensen; *Rally speaker*, Brendan Kelly; *Frankie McVeigh*, James Woods; *Jenny*, Connie Forslund; *Dr. Short*, Robert Gerringer; *Judianne*, Susie Blakely; *Airforce*, Ed Power; *Dumb blonde*, Suzanne Zenor; *Guest*, Dan Seymour.

CREDITS

Produced by Ray Stark; *Directed by* Sydney Pollack; *Written by* Arthur Laurents; *Based upon his novel*; *Photography by* Harry Stradling, Jr., A.S.C.; *Production Designed by* Stephen Grimes; *Edited by* Margaret Booth; *Music by* Marvin Hamlisch; *Song "The Way We Were" composed by* Marvin Hamlisch; *Lyrics by* Marilyn and Alan Bergman; *Sung by* Barbra Streisand; *Costumes by* Dorothy Jeakins, Moss Mabry; *Assistant Director:* Howard Koch, Jr.

(Left) Redford as Hubbell Gardiner and Barbra Streisand as Katie Morosky

SYNOPSIS

Hubbell Gardiner is a handsome, blond WASP college student of the late 1930s. A jock, he is active in school social life and unconcerned with political issues. He wants to be a writer. One of his classmates is Katie Morosky, a Jewish radical involved in various causes including the Young Communists League. She is totally unconcerned with frivolous things like sororities and proms, and has no sense of humor when it comes to politics.

Hubbell's friends continually make fun of Katie, but Hubbell shows her some kindness and shares with her his pleasure at selling his first short story. Later, at

the commencement formal where Katie is serving refreshments, Hubbell asks her to dance and their interest in each other is apparent.

Several years go by, Katie is on radio with political rhetoric, and Hubbell is in the service. They meet accidentally at El Morocco in Manhattan. Hubbell is drunk, and Katie takes him back to her place. He collapses into bed, and she joins him expectantly. His attempts to make love end in his falling asleep on top of her. She whispers to him tearfully, "You did know it was Katie, didn't you?"

Later, Hubbell returns to town and they spend

an evening at Katie's place. She has a copy of a book he had had published, and they discuss his writing. He becomes aware of her sincere interest in his career, and they begin dating. But Hubbell's friends—the same ones he had in college—continue to create problems by joking about the issues Katie feels strongly about. She considers them idiots, and continually makes scenes at parties by telling them off. Hubbell is incensed by Katie's lack of humor, and decides to break off the romance. She wins him back during a tearful exchange in which she explains that she only wants the best for him.

They marry and move to California, where Hubbell is set to turn his novel into a screenplay. Katie protests that he is too good a writer to sell out to movies, but he insists and she gives in. Things go relatively smoothly in Hollywood until the "Red Scare" of the post-WW II era disrupts the film community. Despite Hubbell's insistence against it and her pregnancy, Katie goes to Washington to fight the House Un-American Activities Committee and their hearings.

All of this puts a strain on the Gardiner marriage. Hubbell feels that things are better left alone. He

tells Katie that people are more important than causes, and that after all this is over with, those people accusing each other will be working together. Katie retorts, "Hubbell, people are their principles."

Hubbell is having difficulties at work as well. The film's producers want changes made in Hubbell's script that he doesn't want. He agrees to make them, but begins to feel he is committing the sell-out Katie had warned against. Unsure and depressed, Hubbell spends the night with his ex-girlfriend. Katie finds out about it, and is heartbroken that he would turn to someone she considers so shallow for solace. They realize that their marriage is over. Hubbell tells her, "Katie, what's wrong with us has nothing to do with another woman." They decide to part after the birth of their baby.

Years later, they meet on a New York street. She has remarried and he has become a TV writer. Still in love with each other, they painfully talk about their current lives, realizing that they could never have been happy together. As Katie leaves Hubbell and begins handing out "Ban The Bomb" leaflets, he calls after her, "You never give up, do you?"

The Way We Were was written by Arthur Laurents for Barbra Streisand, with whom he had worked on her first Broadway show in 1962.

Laurents and Ray Stark, who was producing the film and was also a long-time associate of Streisand's, asked Sydney Pollack to direct. They had been impressed with his evocative direction of another period piece, *They Shoot Horses, Don't They?*, which had won him an Oscar nomination in 1969.

Pollack liked the script. "I was very moved by it and I thought right away, Gee, this would be great for Bob." Pollack mentioned to Redford that he was planning to do it and Redford said, "Aw, that piece of junk. Yeah, they sent it to me a long time ago in treatment form. I passed."

Continuing to work on the script, Pollack became convinced that Redford was the only actor who could play Hubbell Gardiner. "When I'd see him I'd drop little hints. I'd say, 'You know this could really be terrific . . . you and Barbra . . . really odd chemistry, you know.' But Redford wouldn't budge."

Pollack finished working on the script and sent it to Redford. He was mystified about Pollack's involvement. "What are you doing this for?" he asked him. "I don't know what you see in this. You must see something in this."

Pollack couldn't convince Redford, and Ray Stark was becoming impatient. He told Pollack, "Look, Ryan O'Neal will do it. We've got Barbra and what do we need Redford for?"

But Pollack would have no one but Redford. "I was ready to pull out of the picture unless I could get Bob,"

he says. "We needed someone strong enough to counter-balance Barbra. She'd been running all over her leading men—no one remembers Omar Sharif in *Funny Girl*, for God's sake—and that just couldn't happen here. The only guy I knew who could just show up and stay with her was Redford. Even O'Neal, who's good and who I like, was lost in their picture together, *What's Up, Doc?* So I knew it just had to be Redford."

Finally, it came down to a confrontation. Stark wanted a definite yes from Redford within one hour or the part would be O'Neal's. "I was in Ray Stark's apartment," says Pollack, "and he was fuming. He said, 'Who does he think he is? I'm not gonna chase my life around Robert Redford'—a real vindictive, ego conversation."

Pollack tried to keep Stark from contacting O'Neal before he had a chance to talk to Redford. He knew Redford had been wavering, because Lola had told Pollack, "I wish he'd make up his mind, already. He's driving me crazy. He sits up at night and says, 'What should I do? I don't like it . . . Pollack is really turned on by it . . . I trust him . . . maybe he sees something I don't see but I don't see it.' "

Pollack went over to Redford's office while Stark waited. He used all his powers of persuasion. He told Redford he wouldn't have to shoot the film for four months—he could take the summer off and spend it with his family in Utah. The film could be shot in New York in the Fall, so Bob could stay with his family when they returned for the children's school terms.

Redford still wanted to know what Pollack saw in the script. "What is this picture about, Pollack? What is this guy? He's just an object . . . he's a nothing . . . he runs around saying, 'Aw, c'mon Katie, c'mon Katie.' He doesn't want anything . . . she wants everything. What does this guy want, Pollack . . . *What does he want?*"

Pollack replied, "He's a very moving guy," and Redford shot back, "What's moving? What's moving?" In the meantime, Stark's secretary was on the phone telling Pollack his hour was up. Stark got on the phone and said, "O.K., come back, we're hiring Ryan O'Neal." "No, you're not," answered Pollack. "Give me ten more minutes."

Finally, Redford put his head in his hands and said, "All right, all right, I'll do it."

"I felt like I'd had another baby," says Pollack. "I called Stark and he said, 'Isn't that wonderful? Congratulations, Sydney'—there was this whole turnaround then."

"The reason I finally decided to do it," says Redford, "was that I had faith that Pollack would make something more out of that character than was in the

Years after college, Katie runs into serviceman Hubbell at El Morocco

The Marx Brothers costume party

original script. Had I not had faith in Sydney and myself and David Rayfiel and Alvin Sargent working together to create some kind of depth to the character, I wouldn't have taken the role. As it was written, he was shallow and one-dimensional. Not very real—more a figment of someone's imagination of what Prince Charming should be like.

"What emerged out of the rewrites were glimpses of the darker side of this golden boy character—what his fears were about himself. The idea was to create a supposed Mr. Perfect but then give little hints along the way that everything wasn't so perfect—or that he, more importantly, knew it wasn't.

"I also felt very strongly, and so did Sydney, that there should be a major confrontation between Katie and Hubbell. In the original script the character was passive all the way through, he was just there for her to love as an object. She loved him and loved him and loved him and then they fell apart—there wasn't any real cataclysmic moment. So we created a massive argument scene in Union Station to give the character a point of view. And that was that, if she were a

person of causes, then he was a people person—people were more important than causes. They were both valid points of view, but Hubbell's wasn't in the original script."

Once filming began at Union College in Schenectady, New York and continued in New York City, no one knew whether the film would turn out well. "The nightmares started quickly," says Pollack. "We were very worried about the script, not only with Bob's character but with how we were going to make the politics work within the framework of the love story. All the time we were filming we were writing, rewriting. It wasn't a pleasant experience.

"Columbia was terribly worried. They were going under at the time, they were changing management, they hadn't had a hit in years. We were way over budget, constantly re-writing. Bob didn't get along with Ray Stark and neither did I. We didn't know how to mix the politics and the love story and make it work. There were just a lot of problems and the whole thing left a bad taste in Bob's mouth."

Though pleased with the Gardiner character as it

Hubbell tells Carol Ann he's moving to California. (With Lois Chiles)

ultimately emerged in the film, Redford isn't happy with the film's politics. "I think it was trying to bring in too much," he says. "It was an interesting device, but it was neither here nor there. It was just a device to break up their marriage. I think the movie could have been achieved without it."

Redford found it somewhat difficult to work with Streisand, and it was the recurring problem of conflicting acting styles. Streisand likes to talk out a scene, and Redford likes to plunge right in. "She'd talk and talk and talk and talk and drive me nuts," he says. "And the amusing thing was that after she'd talk and talk and talk and talk, we'd get down to doing it and she'd do just what she was going to do from the beginning."

As director, Pollack was caught in the middle. "Barbra would call me up every night at nine, ten o'clock and talk about the next day's work for an hour, two hours on the phone. Then she'd get in there and start to talk and Bob would want to do it. And Bob felt the more the talk went, the staler he got. She would feel he was rushing her. The more rehearsing

On location in New York, Redford takes a coffee break

we did, she would begin to go uphill and he would peak and go downhill. So I was like a jockey trying to figure out when to roll the camera and get them to coincide."

"There comes a point when you're ready to go," says Redford. "And then you're better off expending your energies in front of the camera trying things—films are made up of pieces and you might get something usable. But you learn too much in rehearsals. Things start to get pat and film is a medium of behavior and spontaneity."

Despite their stylistic differences, Streisand and Redford had a genuine fondness and respect for each other. "I liked her a lot," says Redford. "I found her very talented, intelligent, insecure and untrusting. Untrusting because she's been told too many lies, she's been hustled, misled, used and jounced by too many hangers-on and hucksters."

Streisand was very impressed with Redford's acting. "She would call me at night," says Pollack, "and say, 'How does he do it?' And she would see the dailies and think that he was wonderful and she stunk. But they're very alike in that respect because he would see them and think she was wonderful and he stunk."

The two stars had many moments of fun together during the filming. "They were always breaking each other up," says Pollack. "It always made her hysterical whenever he said anything Jewish. So there's one scene that's almost all improvised in the beach house in California where he was trying to learn some Jewish words and she was getting hysterical. We just photographed them fooling around and then put it in the film."

For one scene, a costume party in which everyone had to come dressed as a Marx brother, Groucho made a surprise appearance on the set while flashbulbs popped and Redford and Streisand traded fast Marxisms with the comedy great.

But with all the problems surrounding the production of *The Way We Were*, the filming of it was unpleasant for Redford. "He felt he had been made to work in a straitjacket," says Pollack. "And not because of Barbra. Just because of the nature of the film. It was a big expensive picture and we weren't given much freedom. Ray Stark watch-dogged the thing so tightly. . ."

Redford obviously felt great bitterness toward Stark at the end of the filming. At the time he said, "Toward the end of the picture, Sydney began wandering around the sound stage—being on that set was like doing overtime at Dachau. One of the executives on the movie is a loon who has no idea where his head

is. This is one film I want to see, because if this guy has his way, he'll have me cut out of the picture altogether."

He didn't—but Redford, as usual, wasn't at all happy with the final result. "I showed him a rough cut of the picture and he hated himself," says Pollack. "But then he got the first inkling that something was going on the day the picture opened. Lola went by herself. I hadn't even shown her the picture—that's how rough things were. She came home and said, 'It's a very moving picture, Bob—and your work is terrific in it.' And he looked at her and said, 'You're kidding!' "

To the surprise of everyone who went through the problems of filming *The Way We Were*, it became an instantaneous and overwhelming success. The film grossed nearly $34 million in its first three months of release and is now one of Columbia Pictures' three all-time biggest money-makers. Although the film was rapped by critics for its failure to successfully mix the politics with the love story, both stars were praised for their performances and their very special chemistry on screen. And Redford brought to Gardiner more character shadings than were apparent in the script. In many ways, Redford was able to convey more meaning through a simple gesture than through pages of dialogue.

At Academy Award time, Barbra Streisand was nominated for an Oscar as Best Actress, and many Redford fans felt he should have been honored also with a Best Actor nomination. He *was* nominated—but for *The Sting*, a picture released several months later.

More than any film before it, *The Way We Were* changed Robert Redford's life. Millions of people were able to relate to Katie Morosky's idealization of Hubbell Gardiner and Robert Redford became a symbol of sexual desirability, and the biggest male superstar in the world. For the first time, he was named The World Film Favorite (along with Barbra) by the Hollywood Foreign Press Association—largely on the strength of the success of *The Way We Were*. His excessive popularity after *The Way We Were* wasn't something Redford was happy about. "I noticed the difference first in print. I was being labelled a romantic symbol and in many ways it has cut into my ability to be persuasive in other types of roles. I think it's hurt the acting part of my career. And a lot of these articles paint this unreal picture of me as some kind of God. I'm a human being with the same problems and bad aspects as everyone else.

"I don't like to think about it and I don't pay too much attention to it. One thing it has unquestionably done is create great problems of privacy."

REVIEWS

"*The Way We Were* . . . is everything a movie should be: a love story that is a mirror of the hearts of many, a comedy that teeters on the edge of tragedy, a tragedy that teeters on the edge of comedy. Due to the casting, which is nothing short of masterful, the film is vastly superior to the Arthur Laurents novel on which it is based. Barbra Streisand . . . gives the kind of dramatic performance of which Academy Award nominations are made. Robert Redford, as her Hubbell . . . gives a handsomely brooding quality, full of style, to his role . . . The measure of the success of this brilliant motion picture is that it draws the viewer so deeply into its web of character that one is so involved in the dreams and disappointments of its principals that one leaves the theater feeling as one often does when close to a couple who resorts to divorce—wondering 'Which one was right? Which one should I see in the future?' See both Katie and Hubbell again. In *The Way We Were*. It's worth it."

NORMA McLAIN STOOP
After Dark

"One shudders to think what this ponderous romantic drama would have been like without the attractive, redeeming presences of Barbra Streisand and Robert Redford. Even with them *The Way We Were* is borderline entertainment. Can the stars generate enough good will during the first half of the picture to hold viewers through the slow, deadly second hour? . . . Despite its abundant disadvantages, the picture may luck out because Streisand and Redford hit it off so well in the collegiate and courtship scenes. They present such contrasts of temperaments

Katie: "Ya want onions?" Hubbell: "Yeah—in the cokes."

and personalities that their rapport as performers comes as a funny, exhilarating surprise. It's enjoyable to watch them together, especially in the collegiate episodes. Streisand, scrawny and frizzy-haired and intense, makes a peculiarly beautiful, vulnerable image of an ardent coed, and Redford's humorous, diffident responses to her initial envy and hostility are charming and romantically stirring. One feels drawn to both personalities, and one feels the current of sexual curiosity and attraction between them."

GARY ARNOLD

"Pollack and Laurents are so busy working on the dubious proposition that politics can kill a good marriage that they barely have time to establish the political atmosphere that is meant as a catalyst to the connubial collapse, sketching it in hurriedly in bits of cocktail gossip and snippets of radio reports and newspaper headlines. Meanwhile, we watch this luxurious vehicle founder and finally crack apart. Superb performances by Redford and Streisand are not enough to sustain our hopes for the kind of glamorous, big-star romance that Hollywood rarely attempts anymore."

PAUL D. ZIMMERMAN,
Newsweek

"*The Way We Were* is almost a milestone because it's a thoughtful, believable love story for adults. For once, the characters are sharply defined, and their relationship develops and deepens persuasively . . . The differences that attract them will ultimately separate them; but there is real electricity between them . . . Some of the electricity comes from the two stars; their chemistry keeps the movie engaging. Streisand is still too shrill at moments; but this is the most forceful, controlled acting she's ever done. Redford is superb; in scenes where he has little to do except react, he fills in his character with extraordinarily subtle and evocative shadings."

STEPHEN FARBER,
The New York Times (Sunday)

"Redford . . . has rarely been better, and again his gift is being able to suggest the flaws, the weakness, in the heroically handsome figure. The blend of charm, concern and compromise is a subtle shading you find only infrequently in romantic drama."

CHARLES CHAMPLIN,
Los Angeles Times

The Union Station mob scene

"The Switch"

THE STING

A Universal Release of a Bill/Phillips Production (1973). In Technicolor. 129 minutes. Rated PG.

CAST

Henry Gondorff, Paul Newman; *Johnny Hooker,* Robert Redford; *Doyle Lonnegan,* Robert Shaw; *Lt. William Snyder,* Charles Durning; *J. J. Singleton,* Ray Walston; *Crystal,* Sally Kirkland; *Billie,* Eileen Brennan; *Luther Coleman,* Robert Earl Jones; *Kid Twist,* Harold Gould; *Eddie Niles,* John Heffernan; *F.B.I. Agent Polk,* Dana Elcar; *Erie Kid,* Jack Kehoe; *Loretta,* Dimitra Arliss; *Benny Garfield,* Avon Long.

CREDITS

Produced by Tony Bill and Michael and Julia Phillips; *Presented by* Richard A. Zanuck and David Brown; *Directed by* George Roy Hill; *Written by* David S. Ward; *Photography by* Robert Surtees, A.S.C.; *Art Direction by* Henry Bumstead; *Edited by* William Reynolds; *Assistant Director:* Ray Gosnell; *Costumes by* Edith Head; *Music Adapted by* Marvin Hamlisch; *Piano Rags by* Scott Joplin.

Redford as Johnny Hooker, 1930s con man

With Eileen Brennan

Discussing a scene with director George
Roy Hill and Paul Newman

SYNOPSIS

In an alley in Joliet, Illinois in 1936, two men pull off one of the oldest con games—"The Switch" —and are delighted to find that their victim was carrying a big bundle. The money is so much that the older of the two, Luther Coleman, decides to retire and send his young friend Johnny Hooker to Chicago to meet an old crony of his who will teach him to break into the bigtime with "The Big Con."

They soon learn, however, that their victim was a numbers runner for one of the houses run by the formidable Doyle Lonnegan. Coleman is killed and Hooker is on the run. Arriving in Chicago, he finds Coleman's friend, Henry Gondorff, staying at a dismal brothel run by a lady named Billie. They decide to "sting" the man responsible for their friend's death.

They set up a store in a Chicago slum neighborhood, a phony off-track betting joint. Before long, Lt. Snyder, a crooked cop from Joliet, arrives trying to track down Hooker. Hooker is now on the run from Snyder and from Lonnegan's hit men. Then FBI agent Polk shows up looking for Gondorff. Snyder agrees to help Polk get to Hooker, for a fee. Polk tells Hooker he will imprison Hooker and Coleman's widow unless Hooker helps him catch up to Gondorff. Hooker reluctantly agrees, but asks that Polk wait until the "sting" has been accomplished. Polk agrees, figuring the victim deserves what he's going to get. Snyder watches all this, delighted that Hooker has been cornered into betraying his partner.

The sting is set up. After a tip from Hooker, who has convinced Lonnegan he is on his side and wants to break Gondorff, Lonnegan places a $1 million bet on Syphon to win. After the race starts, Lonnegan tells Hooker the bet is safe. Hooker feigns horror and says he meant for Lonnegan to bet the horse to place, not to win. Lonnegan tries to get his money back, but it is too late, the race is on. As the results are being announced, Polk and his men burst in. Polk places Gondorff under arrest, and tells Hooker he is free to go. Realizing his buddy has betrayed him, Gondorff shoots Hooker. Polk in turn shoots Gondorff. Snyder and Lonnegan flee the scene, forgetting about Lonnegan's money.

Once they're gone, Hooker and Gondorff get up, very much alive. Polk was one of Gondorff's men, and the entire scene had been a set-up to make Lonnegan think he was rid of Hooker and Gondorff. The sting is successful.

After the tremendous commercial and critical success of *Butch Cassidy,* it was logical that Redford, Newman and director George Roy Hill would get together again. But the trio never made any efforts toward that end, and, in a fashion which is typical of

With Robert Earl Jones

189

the Redford career, their reunion almost didn't come off.

While Redford was filming *The Way We Were*, Hill approached him to do *The Great Waldo Pepper*, the story of a flying ace of the 1920s. Redford was interested, but *The Way We Were* was running behind schedule. Hill decided to put the filming off for half a year, since the movie could be shot only in the summer months.

In the meantime, Hill was sent a script by David Ward called *The Sting*, about two con men in the Chicago of the 1930s and their efforts to "sting" another con man out of a large sum of money. "I didn't jump up and down and yell 'Eureka!' when I read it," says Hill, "but I liked it and thought it would be good as a filler until I could start *Waldo Pepper*. I also thought Bob would be good for the part of Johnny Hooker."

Hill called Redford about it, and Bob told him he had already read the script and turned it down. "Bob was a little shaky on the script," says Hill, "although he liked it. But the reason he didn't want to do it was that the writer, David Ward, wanted to direct it and Bob wasn't sure he wanted to work with a first-time director on a script he wasn't 100 percent sure about." Once Redford learned that Hill was interested in making the picture, he agreed to play Johnny Hooker.

It never occurred to Hill to have Newman play the other role, that of Gondorff. "The part was originally written as a burly, oafish slob of a man and it was definitely a secondary role," says Hill. "I couldn't see Paul playing it."

But, over lunch in New York, Newman complained to Hill that "you're making another movie with Redford and there's no part for me?" Hill explained his feelings about the Gondorff role but told Newman he could read the script and if he liked the part, it was his.

After reading it, Newman called Hill and agreed that the part wasn't for him. But Hill decided he'd have a little fun. "Because I'm perverse, I started needling him, telling him it was a great part for him and why didn't he do it—I was probably trying to gain points with him later when I could say, 'Look, you turned down that great part in *The Sting*.'"

Several days later, Newman called Hill and said, "I've thought it over—you have yourself an actor." Hill swallowed hard and muttered, "Jesus . . . oh, that's really great."

"What's the matter—are you not anxious?," Newman asked.

"Well, let's not get too hasty. Let's think about it. Let's get together with Redford and talk."

Hill called Redford and told him that he'd offered the part to Newman and he'd accepted. Redford

bellowed, "You couldn't have done that!" Hill explained himself as best he could. "Paul's perfectly aware of the problems so let's go talk with him."

Most of their meeting was spent with Paul listing all the actors who would be better in the role than he. By the time the meeting was over, nothing had been resolved. Finally Hill said, "What the hell are we thinking about? The part can be played as a riverboat gambler. This isn't a classic. We enjoy working together so let's just do it!"

And so it was—with Newman being paid $500,000 plus a percentage of the gross and Redford the same figure minus the percentage—quite a bit more than he'd gotten for *Butch Cassidy*.

The fun and high spirits that characterized the *Butch Cassidy* filming among Redford, Newman and Hill carried over to *The Sting*. There were stunts, challenges, baiting and constant kidding. None of the three allowed any of the others to take himself or the filming too seriously. Hill laughs merrily as he relates one story of Redford discontent. "Bob chomped at the bit a lot during the filming because, since it was an enormously complicated plot piece, he had a tremendous number of scenes where he was required to carry the plot. He complained that all he seemed to be doing was showing up and saying, 'You meet me at the corner of Ninth and Fifth and I'll telephone the guy at Eighth and Sixth and then we'll cross the street and the bell will ring four times and . . .'

"One day he started yelling at me, 'This isn't acting—I'm just carrying the plot around on a dolly. Every time I come in there's a five minute pause while I explain to the audience what the hell is going on!' Of course," Hill smiles mischievously as he continues, "Paul was sitting around collecting the gravy, because he never had to explain a word of plot."

Redford has a great deal of respect for Hill as a director. "He's a great storyteller. If he has a good story to tell, his work is inclined to be better—he doesn't go in as much for character study as other directors, like Pollack. He's very demanding, a tremendous disciplinarian and a taskmaster. That becomes stimulating in itself—working for someone who's constantly challenging you to do the job as well as it can be done. The implication with George is that it can always be done better. He runs a very professional set—as a matter of fact, it's like being in a bomber squadron."

Once filming of *The Sting* was completed, Hill was a little reluctant to show it to Redford, knowing of his penchant for disliking himself on screen. "When I showed him *Butch Cassidy*," Hill says, "I sat behind him in the screening room and watched his head sink lower and lower into the seat as the movie progressed. I thought to myself, I don't need this, so I left. And I

With Dimitra Arliss

With Robert Shaw and Paul Newman

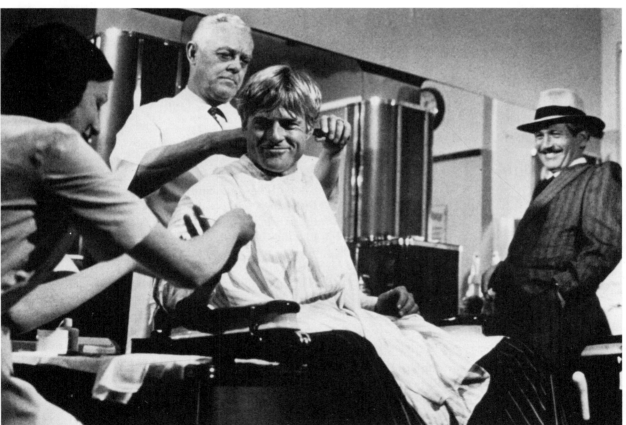

Hooker gets a haircut (with Paul Newman)

wasn't about to go through that again with *The Sting*."

Redford, though more critical on himself than was warranted, liked *The Sting*; it was clear that Redford, Newman, Hill and Co. had made quite a special movie. It was a fun film, with Newman and Redford playing each other off with all the charm and buoyancy they could muster. The film was praised by critics as superior to *Butch Cassidy,* and it soon became clear that *The Sting* would outgross that film considerably.

With *The Way We Were* and *The Sting* breaking box office records and Redford's next picture *The Great Gatsby* garnering more advance publicity than any film since *Cleopatra,* Robert Redford was riding a crest of public adulation rarely seen even in hype-weary Hollywood. The Redford mania, though, was genuine. If women responded to him as a sex symbol in *The Way We Were,* men could relate to the brotherly comaraderie between Redford and Newman in *The Sting*. Robert Redford was in the unusual position of appealing to practically everyone at the same time.

Two months after its release, *The Sting* was nominated for ten Academy Awards, among them Robert Redford as Best Actor. Redford didn't think he deserved the award, and couldn't understand why Newman hadn't been nominated as well. He had never been too impressed by Oscars, anyway. "It seemed like an awful lot of extravagance for nothing. And the awards were always being won by people who had done better work before, or did better work later. The Oscars just reflect the opinion of Academy members. The guy who wins an award for a foot race gets it because he was the fastest guy on that track at that moment. That's the only kind of race I have any respect for."

Still, Redford was flattered. "To a certain extent I was honored because I realize there *are* people who do care about the awards. But when I didn't win, I was relieved. I just didn't deserve it."

The film, however, cleaned up at Oscar time. It won seven awards, including Best Picture of 1973, and Best Director. Not bad for a film that was made as a "filler" while Hill and Redford waited to do *The Great Waldo Pepper*.

REVIEWS

"The casting is perfect. Who could better play two slick con men hustling their way through the Depression than Paul Newman and Robert Redford? For Newman and Redford are masters of the con. With their charismatic, effortless charm, they can have an audience eating out of the palms of their hands without even trying. Just one of their winning smiles (particularly Redford's bright smiles) and it's all over. The audience will follow them anywhere; through the worst of movies, through the best of them, it doesn't matter which. And so *The Sting* works, not because of the tart script (that leaves characterization entirely up to the actors); not because of director George Roy Hill's all-out effort to give the movie a period flavor, but because it has Newman and Redford, the best male team in films . . . They have developed a form of instant communication. Words are not as important as the way they look at each other. Call it a snow job or call it acting, it is very pleasing to watch."

KATHLEEN CARROLL,
New York Daily News

"*The Sting* reunites the screen's leading romantic couple—Paul Newman and Robert Redford—directed once again by George Roy Hill, who made *Butch Cassidy and the Sundance Kid* . . . Like its heroes, the film succeeds on charm and con. Newman and Redford radiate a charismatic appeal that tilts the movie in their favor . . . This is the kind of commercially infallible film that a director dare not fiddle with. His job is to bring the material to the screen with care and clarity—nothing more—and George Roy Hill does his job, nothing more. The result lacks the emancipating energy of *Butch Cassidy*. For all its charm, *The Sting* has the slightly stale, carefully crafted feel of a sure-fire sequel. But who can argue, when this lightweight delight is destined to make many millions, and artistic adventurousness might only have sent it down the drain?"

PAUL D. ZIMMERMAN,
Newsweek

"Paul Newman and Robert Redford are wonderfully convincing (and droll) as two practitioners of the gentle art of separating a sucker from his money, playing the game with purposeful charm, insouciant good humor and persuasive flimflammery. That they are unmitigated, conscienceless scoundrels enjoying every ploy of the big con is of secondary consideration; after all, their intent is commendable and there is no harm in cheating a cheater, especially when the cheater is Robert Shaw, who stalks through the deception with exquisite nastiness. I realize this is not a recommended moral attitude. However, in today's world, I am often led to wonder what is."

MILTON KRIMS,
Saturday Evening Post

196

With Robert Shaw and Charles
Dierkop

"Zillions of moviegoers who flipped for *Butch Cassidy* will no doubt perform handsprings in response to this old-fashioned yarn . . . Playing the senior member of the team, Newman has none of the self-conscious cuteness that so often cramps his comic style—while Redford, as the junior partner, also hangs loose to burnish his image as one of the brightest comets to light up the Hollywood sky since Grant and Gable went West. David S. Ward's scenario defies the laws of credibility, though any kind of lawbreaking seems reasonable after a while in this wonderland of wickedness."

Playboy

"*The Sting* looks and and sounds like a musical comedy from which the songs have been removed, leaving only a background score of old-fashioned, toe-tapping piano rags that as easily evoke the pre-World War I teens as the nineteen-thirties. A lot of the other period details aren't too firmly anchored in time, but the film is so goodnatured, so obviously aware of everything it's up to, even its own pictur-esque frauds, that I opt to go along with it. One forgives its unrelenting efforts to charm, if only because *The Sting* itself is a kind of con game, devoid of the poetic aspirations that weighed down *Butch Cassidy and the Sundance Kid.*

"The only woman with a substantial role in the film is Eileen Brennan . . . *The Sting* is not the kind of film that takes its women very seriously, and the continuing popularity of these male-male co-starring teams should, I suppose, probably prompt some solemn analysis. It is not, I suspect, a terrible perversion of the romantic movie-team concept idealized by William Powell and Myrna Loy, Clark Gable and Lana Turner but, rather a variation on the old Dr. Gillespie–Dr. Kildare relationship, with a bit of Laurel and Hardy

thrown in. It is also apparently very good box office."

VINCENT CANBY
The New York Times

"This isn't a movie, it's a recipe. The people who put *The Sting* together followed the instructions on the *Butch Cassidy* package: one Paul Newman, one Robert Redford, a dash of caper. Stir in the same director, if available. He was. *Butch Cassidy* may not have been very good, but it made a bundle, so what difference does it make? Newman and Redford pass a few facial expressions between them and try to cool each other out. If there ever was much of a script, it can be said to have gone to waste . . . *The Sting* was not made to be taken seriously, but many people may find it difficult even to enjoy the movie casually. It lacks the elements that could give it a true drive: a sense of an urban underworld, or of the Depression that sucked so many people into it; an understanding of the con man's pathology that goes beyond surface style and patter; a story that depends not on plot twists but on characters. The movie ends up with a lot of expensive sets and a screenful of blue eyes."

JAY COCKS,
Time

"Paul Newman and Robert Redford make an unbeatable team of charismatic performers, especially when they are up to no good, as is the case in this elaborately worked out, suspenseful comedy . . . It is light, frothy entertainment of the highest order, but the fact that it is primarily a fun picture didn't stop director Hill from imbuing it with the most sophisticated atmospheric detail, thereby raising its level above sheer escapism . . ."

WILLIAM WOLF,
Cue

With Mia Farrow

THE GREAT GATSBY

A Paramount Release (1974). In Panavision and Color. 146 minutes. Rated **PG**.

CAST

Jay Gatsby, Robert Redford; *Daisy Buchanan,* Mia Farrow; *Tom Buchanan,* Bruce Dern; *Myrtle Wilson,* Karen Black; *George Wilson,* Scott Wilson; *Nick Carraway,* Sam Waterston; *Jordan Baker,* Lois Chiles; *Meyer Wolfsheim,* Howard DaSilva; *Mr. Gatz,* Roberts Blossom; *Klipspringer,* Edward Herrmann; *Wilson's Friend,* Elliot Sullivan; *Dog Vendor,* Arthur Hughes; *Catherine,* Kathryn Leigh Scott; *Mrs. McKee,* Beth Porter; *Mr. McKee,* Paul Tamarin; *Gatsby's Bodyguard,* John Devlin; *Pamela Buchanan,* Patsy Kensit; *Pamela's Nurse,* Marjorie Wildes; *Reporter,* Jerry Mayer; *Detectives at Pool,* Bob Sherman, Norman Chauncer; *Miss Baedeker,* Regina Baff; *Twins,* Janet Arters, Louise Arters; *Fat Man,* Oliver Clark; *Thin Man,* Vincent Schiavelli; *Comic,* Sammy Smith; *Special Appearance by* Tom Ewell.

CREDITS

Directed by Jack Clayton; *Produced by* David Merrick; *Screenplay by* Francis Ford Coppola; *Based on the novel by* F. Scott Fitzgerald; *Associate Producer* Hank Moonjean; *Photography by* Douglas Slocombe; *Music Supervised by* Nelson Riddle; *Production Designed by* John Box; *Costumes by* Theoni V. Aldredge; *Assistant Directors:* David Tringham, Alex Hapsas; *Art Directors:* Eugene Rudolf, Robert Laing; *Choreographer:* Tony Stevens; *Edited by* Tom Priestly; *Arrangements and Additional Music Composed and Conducted by* Nelson Riddle.

SYNOPSIS

Nick Carraway lives in a small house next to the elegant mansion owned by a mysterious man named Jay Gatsby. Nick is friends with Tom Buchanon and his wife Daisy, who is also a distant cousin of Nick's. Visiting the Buchanans, Nick meets Daisy's attractive friend Jordan Baker.

Tom takes Nick to meet his mistress Myrtle, who lives with her husband above a run-down auto-repair shop. Myrtle's husband George suspects his wife's infidelity, but is too weak to do anything about it. Myrtle, Tom and Nick go to an apartment Tom keeps for parties.

Each night, Gatsby's house is the scene of a lavish party, but Gatsby is never seen. Attending one of them, Nick is invited up to meet Gatsby, who turns out to be a polite, reserved, somewhat awkward man of new wealth. Gatsby takes Nick to lunch one day and Nick meets a racketeer named Wolfsheim. Nick senses that Wolfsheim and Gatsby were involved in some shady dealings...

Gatsby confides in Nick that he has long been in love with Daisy, whom he was once supposed to marry. He asks Nick to set up a reunion between them, which Nick does. In a romantic, flowered setting in Nick's house, the two meet again, both nervous and afraid. They renew their romance and Gatsby blossoms into sociability.

Trouble begins when Tom accuses Gatsby of trying to steal his wife. When Gatsby is returning home from an outing to the city, his car strikes Myrtle in front of the shop and she is killed. Daisy was driving the car, but Gatsby takes the blame for the accident.

George, in his grief, sets out to revenge Myrtle's death and shoots Gatsby, then himself.

Gatsby's funeral is attended only by Nick and Gatsby's father. The father tells Nick that Gatsby's life was a long quest for riches that would help him to win Daisy. She had left him and married Tom because Gatsby wasn't rich enough.

Ever since F. Scott Fitzgerald's novel *The Great Gatsby* first appeared in 1925, Hollywood has longed to transfer it successfully to the screen. The first two such attempts, in 1926 and 1949, were commercial and artistic failures and, for twenty-three years after the second version, the conventional wisdom was that the classic romantic tale was "unfilmable."

The very things that made *The Great Gatsby* an enormously entertaining reading experience worked against it whenever an attempt was made to film it. The brooding, mysterious persona of Gatsby, the pervading romantic melancholy of his quest to find his lost love, and the basically thin plot line gave *The*

With Mia Farrow

Mia Farrow as Daisy Buchanan, Redford as Jay Gatsby

The Great *Gatsby* fashion hype

With Mia Farrow

Confrontation—with Bruce Dern,
Sam Waterston, Mia Farrow and
Lois Chiles

Great Gatsby an ethereal quality. So much was left to the reader's imagination that any crystallization of characters and locales disappointed the majority of the book's followers.

By 1972, however, America was in the midst of a nostalgia craze; the previous *Gatsby* failures were forgotten and Ali MacGraw, a longtime fan of the book, wanted to play Daisy. MacGraw, who had been Oscar-nominated for the immensely popular *Love Story*, was married to Bob Evans, Paramount Pictures' production chief. Evans went to successful Broadway producer David Merrick and told him, "I want to do this picture for Ali, and I think you have the class to do it properly."

The film rights had reverted to Fitzgerald's daughter, Scottie Smith, and Evans had hoped to buy them for $130,000. But by the time Merrick got to Mrs. Smith, word of Paramount's interest had leaked out and sparked competition from a number of other bidders, Ray Stark and Robert Redford among them. Merrick won out a year and a half later, paying Mrs. Smith $350,000 plus a good percentage of the film's profits.

Now the search for someone to play Gatsby began. Warren Beatty and Jack Nicholson were considered and both were interested, but only if Ali MacGraw, whose reputation as an actress was not legendary, did not play Daisy. That was out of the question for Evans, who next turned to Marlon Brando. He wanted too much money. The fact that Brando was fifty and Gatsby is thirty-one didn't seem to bother anyone at Paramount. Redford said later, "The fact that Paramount approached Marlon really makes you wonder. Didn't anyone there bother to read the book?"

Redford was the next actor approached, and Paramount didn't have to go any further. "I wanted Gatsby badly," he says. "He is not fleshed out in the book, and the implied parts of his character are fascinating." Redford saw the part as another challenge for him —"It was a chance to elude a stereotyped image."

The next step in the Gatsby saga was finding a director. Peter Bogdanovich, Arthur Penn and Mike Nichols were interested, but they too were opposed to Ali MacGraw's playing Daisy. British director Jack Clayton was finally signed, although he hadn't made a movie in seven years and many spectators wondered whether anyone but an American could do justice to so American a tale.

Getting the screenplay into shape was next on the agenda, and Truman Capote was hired. But his treatment was rejected by Paramount as "unacceptable." Word had it that he turned Nick into a homosexual and Jordan into a lesbian. Capote sued Paramount for breach of contract when they rejected his

scenario, and they made an out-of-court settlement of $110,000.

Francis Ford Coppola was then given the assignment, and in three weeks he turned in the script which was finally used—with, according to Merrick, a good deal of help from Jack Clayton. "Clayton should get co-author credit," he says, "but the Screen Writers Guild counts the number of words and that determines who gets credit on the screen. They don't give credit for construction, polishing or creative work that is not actually seen on the screen."

The production seemed all ready to go at this point —until a huge monkey wrench was thrown into the works. Ali MacGraw and Bob Evans were heading for a divorce because of her involvement with Steve McQueen, her leading man in *The Getaway*. Evans pulled out of the production, leaving David Merrick as the sole producer. But Evans, as production chief of Paramount, still had a finger in the *Gatsby* pie.

Merrick picks up the narrative from here. "The scene then shifts to a phone call I got from Freddie Fields at CMA. He asked me, 'How would you feel about Steve McQueen playing Gatsby?' I said, 'Red-

With Sam Waterson

quickly became the most pre-sold movie in history. Frank Yablans saw it as completing a "triple crown" begun by the phenomenal success for Paramount of *Love Story* and *The Godfather*. Paramount embarked on a grand design to "Gatsbyize" America, and got a push in that effort by *Women's Wear Daily*, which dubbed a new line of clothes "The Gatsby Look." Sensing a fashion trend in the air, Paramount contracted carefully with four major companies for Gatsby tie-ins: Glemby Hair Salons ("After you've seen *The Great Gatsby*, get the cut"); Robert Bruce Sportswear for men; Ballantine's "21" Brands Scotch and E.I. duPont, which marketed "Classic White" Teflon cookware "in the tradition of *The Great Gatsby*."

The promotional tie-ins were worth $6 million, and the whole thing left Scottie Smith somewhat aghast. "I think Daddy would have loved being a Teflon pan more than anything else," she joked.

The *Gatsby* "hype," while praised by Bob Evans ("the making of a blockbuster is the newest art form of the Twentieth Century") left a bad taste in Robert Redford's mouth. He'd have no part of any exploitation ("Drape me in a suit like a *Vogue* model? No way!") and felt the expectations of everyone put a tremendous strain on the cast. "It was like being in a straitjacket for 18 weeks," he says.

During the filming, Redford's double-header of *The Way We Were* and *The Sting* focused a great deal of attention on him and furthered the expectation that *Gatsby* would be a smash. Redford, unhappy with the constraints of a difficult role and submerged in his interpretation, didn't take too kindly to the constant demand from newsmen for interviews and quotes. One irate journalist saw Redford with daughter Amy and muttered, "Daughter, hell. He got that kid from rent-a-child just to keep the press off his back."

Redford dyed his hair brown for the role. "I wasn't happy about it," he says, "but in retrospect I think it was a good idea, because it helped me feel slightly awkward, and an important part of Gatsby's character, it seems to me, was his awkwardness—and the attempts he made to conceal it."

By the time filming was completed in London early in 1974, Paramount's "making of a blockbuster" was complete. The film had an unprecedented $18.6 million in advance bookings on the pre-publicity alone, and since it had cost $6.4 million, it was a profitable film before a single viewer had seen it. As things turned out, had Paramount not mounted the campaign it did, *The Great Gatsby* would have been a commercial disaster.

Perhaps because most critics found the "hype" so offensive, the reviews of *The Great Gatsby* were harsh and, in some cases, vicious. *Newsweek* said Clayton

ford is signed for the part and we're very happy with him.' He said, 'Well, you could find another part for Redford and give McQueen the lead. That's the only way you'll get Ali, because McQueen won't allow her to be in it unless he plays Gatsby.' I wouldn't even consider it, so Ali asked for a release. She lost her husband and the picture."

The search for a new Daisy began, accompanied by the appropriate press ballyhoo. Established actresses like Faye Dunaway, Candice Bergen and Katharine Ross were being subjected to highly unusual screen tests when Evans got a cable from Mia Farrow in London: "Dear Bob, may I be your Daisy?" Clayton tested her in London and the entire production team of Clayton, Merrick, Evans, Frank Yablans (president of Paramount) and Charles Bluhdorn agreed that Mia brought to Daisy a quality they had been searching for. "She had an aristocratic look," says Merrick, and Evans adds, "She brought a mystical quality, a kind of spoiled arrogance, that made her especially interesting."

The filming of *The Great Gatsby* began at Newport, Rhode Island amid a swirl of publicity. It

THE GREAT WALDO PEPPER

A Universal Pictures Release of a Jennings Lang Presentation (1975). In Technicolor. 107 minutes. Rated PG.

CAST

Waldo Pepper, Robert Redford; *Axel Olsson*, Bo Svenson; *Ernst Kessler*, Bo Brundin; *Mary Beth*, Susan Sarandon; *Newt*, Geoffrey Lewis; *Ezra Stiles*, Edward Herrmann; *Dillhoefer*, Philip Bruns; *Werfel*, Roderick Cook; *Patsy*, Kelly Jean Peters; *Maude*, Margot Kidder.

CREDITS

Produced and Directed by George Roy Hill; *Screenplay by* William Goldman; *Story by* George Roy Hill; *Associate Producer:* Robert L. Crawford; *Director of Photography:* Robert Surtees, A.S.C.; *Art Director:* Henry Bumstead; *Set Decorations:* James Payne; *Sound:* Bob Miller, Ronald Pierce; *Sound Effects Editor:* Peter Berkos, M.P.S.E.; *Film Editor:* William Reynolds, A.C.E.; *Costumes by* Edith Head; *Music:* Henry Mancini; *Air Sequences Supervised by* Frank Tallman; *Air Work by* Tallmantz Aviation: James S. Appleby, Wayne Berg, Howard Curtis, Mike Dewey, John Kazian, Thomas Mooney, Frank Pine, Frank Price, Audrey Saunders, Art Scholl, Frank Tallman, Ralph Wiggins; *Casting:* Marion Dougherty Associates; *Camera Operator:* Chuck Short; *Script Supervisor:* Charlsie Bryant; *Costume Supervisor:* Bernard Pollack; *Makeup:* Gary Liddiard; *Unit Production Manager:* Lloyd Anderson; *First Assistant Director:* Ray Gosnell; *Second Assistant Director:* Jerry Ballew; *Still Photographs Courtesy of* Hatfield History of Aeronautics; *Titles & Optical Effects:* Universal Title; *Cosmetics by* Cinematique.

With Philip Bruns

SYNOPSIS

For some of the pilots returning from World War I, flying had become an exhilarating life. But the only way to fly in the 1920s was to "barnstorm"—fly from town to town doing daredevil stunts and offering local farmers quick and exciting rides.

One of these "flying aces" is Waldo Pepper, who is upset when he arrives in a town and learns that Axel Olsson is already milking the market. Waldo removes the wheels from Axel's plane, forcing him to crash land. Axel retaliates by moving in on Waldo with Mary Beth and exposing as a lie Waldo's story about flying against the legendary German ace Ernst Kessler.

Axel and Waldo go to Doc Dillhoefer, who runs a flying circus. Doc tells them he wants acts, not stunts, so Mary Beth convinces the two rivals to team up. Their first act, a car-to-plane transfer—results in severe injuries to Waldo, who winds up in several casts. Waldo recuperates at his friend Ezra's house and a romance blossoms between him and Ezra's sister Maude. Waldo is interested in financing a new monoplane that Ezra has been developing. He believes that with this plane he can perform the last untried stunt: the outside loop.

Back in action, Waldo rejoins Axel and they develop a wing-walking routine. Once the novelty wears off, they enlist Mary Beth as the "IT Girl of the Skies." Her first attempt to wing-walk ends fatally. The tragedy forces Newton Pipp, a government air inspector, to ground Waldo and Axel. Ezra decides to take his new plane up himself, and he completes the outside loop successfully. But then the plane's wings fold in and he crashes. A morbidly curious crowd gathers and Waldo scatters them with his low flying plane. Dozens of people are hurt in the ensuing panic, and Waldo is permanently grounded.

Waldo goes back to Maude and thinks of settling down. But he soon realizes that he must fly, and, using an assumed name, goes to Hollywood where Axel is working as a movie stunt man. Waldo gets a job flying in a movie about Ernst Kessler's life. Kessler is there, set to do his own flying. There is an unspoken bond of respect between Kessler and Waldo. Waldo sees this as his chance to really have that dogfight with Kessler he had told Mary Beth about.

The two men go up and give the director the footage he needs. But they ignore his orders to descend and begin a gritty, to-the-finish dogfight. It is soon clear that Waldo has won. He gives Kessler a symbolic salute—the same one Kessler gave his opponent in the war thirteen years earlier.

George Roy Hill conceived the idea of doing a movie about barnstorming flyers of the 1920s while filming *Thoroughly Modern Millie* in 1965. An air-

Redford as The Great Waldo Pepper, 1920s flying ace

210

2069-6

plane enthusiast and licensed pilot, Hill was fascinated by the saga of these men, who eked out a living flying from town to town, giving sky rides and thrilling the populace with their dare-devil aerobatics. "These men provided the bridge between two eras," says Hill. "Many of them paved the way for commercial aviation as we know it today."

It wasn't until November of 1973, however, that Hill started to film his pet project, with Robert Redford in the title role of Waldo Pepper. "I'm making this movie for fun," said Redford. "Like *The Sting*. It has no message. It should be very entertaining and have a sense of style, adventure and romance."

Hill acknowledges that the romantic, adventuresome spirit of Waldo Pepper appealed to Redford. "Before we started the picture I took him up in my plane and did just about every conceivable aerobatic stunt with it, and he loved it. He really freaked on it."

Getting the daredevil flying stunts and a movie-ending dogfight on film wasn't nearly as much fun, however. In Texas for the flying sequences, Hill was faced with a myriad of logistical problems in trying to get realistic flight footage. Licensed pilots were actually flying the planes Redford was supposedly in control of. They had to fly the plane blind, pinned under machine guns, while a sighted camera made it appear as though Redford, in the rear cockpit, was flying the plane. The difficulty of doing this was apparent when one pilot was mangled in a crash and Frank Tallman, who supervised the air sequences, was seriously injured when his plane flew into some high-tension wires.

Hill took every possible precaution to insure maximum safety. "I pretty well knew what the limits were, and we went right up to the limits of being safe. I didn't ask anyone to do anything I wouldn't have done myself. I did go out on the wing of the plane and stand up in the back cockpit—not so much to prove that it could be done but to prove that the camera would work and that the angles were right."

Quite a bit of ballyhoo attended the news that Robert Redford, the most valuable property in Hollywood, had actually wing-walked 3,000 feet above the ground during a scene in which he climbs from one plane to another. Frank Tallman marveled, "Redford's the gutsiest guy I've ever worked with. Not even Doug Fairbanks walked the wing of a plane in flight!" Redford says, "I felt incredible freedom. But then I thought—What am I doing here?"

"We had to have him do it for the sake of realism," says Hill. "We had Redford walk out to the first bay, but as soon as he got there we cut and the stuntman took over. There was no point in pressing our luck. For the scene where he reaches up to the passing plane to transfer, I had him stand up in the back cockpit of the plane I was filming from so it would look like he was doing it from the edge of a wing."

Redford admits all this had him "cosmically terrified," but Hill will only go so far as to say that Redford was "uncomfortable" around airplanes. "He wasn't nervous, just uneasy. The thing was, if anything happened to the pilot while we were filming Redford, he couldn't have taken over the controls because he didn't know how to fly. This feeling of helplessness kind of spooked him, because he always likes to be in control."

Hill smiles as he recalls that it was sometimes difficult to get Redford into the plane. "I could have made an entire movie if I'd counted the number of minutes it used to take for him to get from his dressing room to the plane. He'd conduct business, pick out a scarf, try on four pairs of gloves, using every device possible to avoid the moment when he had to get into the airplane. But he did it, and my hat's off to him for it."

Interiors on *Waldo Pepper* were completed at Universal's Burbank studios. For the film's premiere in March of 1975, Redford—as he had done for just a few films before it—broke his rule about not attending premieres of his films. The New York opening was a benefit for Lola's group, Consumer Action Now, and there was a picnic and auction following the screening.

The critical reaction to *The Great Waldo Pepper* was mixed, praise being reserved primarily for the action sequences and Redford's smile. Though likable enough as entertainment, the film will probably not be one of Robert Redford's more memorable efforts.

REVIEWS

"*Waldo Pepper* is a flamboyant movie, eminently satisfying just as a spectacle. What transforms it into something more is the authenticity that director Hill, whose avocation is flying antique airplanes, brings to it. He is obviously paying tribute to a spirit of gallantry that he believes in and admires. Fortunately, he has communicated his earnestness to writer Goldman, whose humor is tempered by uncharacteristic restraint, and to an excellent cast, among whom Bo Brundin as Kessler stands out. As for Redford, this is his best work since *Downhill Racer*. Appealingly awkward when trying to express his feeling for flying, he is in his most dashingly self-destructive mode when demonstrating the heights to which his passion drives him. All in all, *The Great Waldo Pepper* is popular entertainment of a very high order."

RICHARD SCHICKEL,
Time

"These days, all Robert Redford has to do is smile. Put him in 1920s airplanes, have him do some barnstorming, stunt flying and a bit of roguish romancing on the side, and you are bound to have a film with a fair share of entertainment. Director Hill tried for something more than that, but his film flight-pattern got lost between light-headed Hollywood corn and the intended sophistication. . . . William Goldman's screenplay is loaded with movieland coincidence. Redford, Bo Svenson as his buddy, Susan Sarandon and Margot Kidder are appealing to watch, but are locked into the unreality. The role of Kessler, milked by Bo Brundin, is so cliched it borders on camp.

"Hill pulls off some dandy vintage flying sequences. That aspect alone has charm, professionalism and visual excitement. But Hill and Goldman fail in their try at turning the corner toward serious depiction of the driven men. The strained solemnity saddles the entertainment elements with a downbeat feeling—but without the required dramatic rewards."

WILLIAM WOLF,
Cue

Tragedy strikes the air show

Waldo becomes a movie stunt man

Lola visits her husband on location

Waldo recuperates from an accident
(with Margo Kidder)

With Susan Sarandon

"Goldman, Hill and Redford are after something more than *The Hardy Boys Go Flying*, but instead of creating characters and relationships we can care about, they go for Big Themes: Hero vs. The Bureaucrats, the exploitation of stunt flyers by Hollywood and, of course, the Meaning of Life. Overloaded with such heavy thinking, the movie nosedives."

PAUL D. ZIMMERMAN,
Newsweek

"*The Great Waldo Pepper* is an uneven and unsatisfying story of anachronistic, pitiable, but misplaced heroism, a handsome period film that wavers uncertainly between comedy and drama, leaving its philosophical ideas ragged and dangling. Redford's current marquee boom and the nostalgia wave may create some box office action, but results could be spotty. . . . With technological resources at hand that Howard Hughes, Howard Hawks and William Wellman never possessed when they made some historic aerial-themed films, Hill has labored mightily to produce a comparative mouse, a soggy paean to a child-man."

MURF.,
Variety

"Redford, as a maverick pilot, has never looked better. He is almost too blond, too beautiful, too good to be true. Sure, this movie is gossamer, romantic fluff for those of us who admire Redford's considerable acting talents. Meantime, *Waldo Pepper* gives you an evening of Redford—what's not to like?"

LIZ SMITH,
Cosmopolitan

THREE DAYS OF THE CONDOR

A Paramount Release of a Wildwood Enterprise Co-production (1975) In Technicolor and Panavision. Rated R.

CAST

Turner, Robert Redford; *Kathy,* Faye Dunaway; *Higgins,* Cliff Robertson; *Joubert,* Max Von Sydow; *Mr. Wabash,* John Houseman; *Atwood,* Addison Powell; *Barber,* Walter McGinn; *Janice,* Tina Chen; *Wicks,* Michael Kane; *Dr. Lappe,* Don McHenry; *Fowler,* Michael Miller; *Mitchell,* Jess Osuna; *Thomas,* Dino Narizzano; *Mrs. Russell,* Helen Stenborg; *Martin,* Patrick Gorman; *Jennings,* Hansford Rowe, Jr.; *Mae Barber,* Carlin Glynn; *Mailman,* Hank Garrett; *Messenger,* Arthur French; *Tall Thin Man,* Jay Devlin; *Jimmy,* Frank Savino; *Newberry,* Robert Phalen; *Beefy Man,* John Randolph Jones; *Hutton,* Garrison Phillips; *Heidegger,* Lee Steele; *Ordinance Man,* Ed Crowley; *TV Reporter,* John Connell; *Alice Lieutenant,* Norman Bush.

CREDITS

Directed by Sydney Pollack; *Produced by* Stanley Schneider; *Screenplay by* Lorenzo Semple, Jr. and David Rayfiel; *Based on the Novel "Six Days of the Condor" by* James Grady; *Director of Photography:* Owen Roizman; *Music by* Dave Grusin; *Production Design:* Stephen Grimes; *Art Director:* Gene Rudolf; *Ms. Dunaway's Clothes:* Theoni V. Aldredge; *Production Manager:* Paul Ganapoler; *1st Assistant Director:* Pete Scoppa; *2nd Assistant Directors:* Mike Haley, Ralph Singleton, Kim Kurumada; *Production Services:* Condor Production Company; *Supervising Film Editor:* Frederic Steinkamp; *Film Editor:* Don Guidice; *Assistant to Producer:* Federico De Laurentiis; *Casting:* Shirley Rich; *Set Decorator:* George De Titta; *Proper Manager:* Allan Levine; *Special Effects:* Augie Lohman; *Master Scenic:* Bruno Robotti; *Gaffer:* Dusty Wallace; *Key Grip:* Robert Ward.

Redford as Joe Turner, a CIA reader caught up in events he doesn't understand

Turner survives the mailman's assassination attempt (with Hank Garrett and Faye Dunaway)

Faye Dunaway and Redford on the set

SYNOPSIS

Joseph Turner is a reader for Manhattan's American Literary Historical Society, which is actually a front for the CIA. Turner and his co-workers read, analyze and computerize popular fiction as part of the agency's intelligence gathering operation.

Turner is disappointed to learn that an inquiry he had made into what seemed to be an intriguing irregularity has turned out to be of no importance at headquarters. Later, returning with his co-workers' lunches, he finds them all brutally murdered.

Horrified, he calls Headquarters and identifies himself by his code name, Condor. Deputy Director Higgins tells him to meet another agent behind the Ansonia Hotel. Agent Wicks will meet him there with Turner's friend Sam Barber, sent along so that Turner will know them. When Turner shows up, Wicks tries to shoot him and kills Barber. Turner shoots Wicks in the leg and flees.

Confused, Turner abducts a young woman, Kathy Hale, and makes her take him to her apartment. In Washington, a meeting is held at which CIA leaders and top members of the Joint Chiefs of Staff try to figure things out. Why was such an insignificant section hit? Why did Turner shoot Barber and Wicks? When the session ends, CIA man Atwood meets secretly with Joubert, who has carried out the killings of Turner's co-workers, and tells him to kill Turner and Wicks.

Turner binds and gags Kathy and visits Sam's widow. Joubert has anticipated this move and the two share an elevator. Turner is suspicious and manages to get away, but Joubert gets the license number of Kathy's car.

Back at Kathy's, Turner and the girl make love. The next morning, a mailman tries to assassinate Turner, but Turner kills him. A piece of paper in the dead man's pocket links him to Wicks.

Turner decides to see Higgins in person. Kathy lures him into her car and Turner, pointing a gun, asks Higgins what is going on. Turner thinks it has something to do with his inquiry, which was why a mystery novel had been translated into only Dutch and Arabic. Higgins doesn't know, and when Turner suggests he ask Wicks, Higgins tells him Wicks is dead.

Higgins finds a link in the pasts of Joubert and Wicks. Turner traces Joubert to a hotel through a key he found on the mailman. He is able to tap Joubert's phone while Joubert is calling Atwood in Washington, and he decides to go there to find out who Atwood is.

Turner breaks into Atwood's home, and gets an answer. Atwood had set up an unauthorized intelligence system within the CIA to help the U.S. gain influence in the oil-producing countries. Turner's

*inquiry threatened to reveal the covert section and
thus the Literary Society had to be wiped out. Joubert
appears and kills Atwood, telling Turner he now
works for the CIA and was ordered to get rid of
Atwood. He tells Turner to join him, because he
seems to have a knack for CIA work.*

*Turner refuses and confronts Higgins in New York.
Higgins tries to bring him back to the fold, but
Turner will have none of it and informs Higgins he
has given the entire story to* The New York Times.
*Higgins says that if they don't run it, Turner will be
in big trouble. But Turner has done what he had to
do.*

Co-workers Joe and Janice (with Tina Chen)

Not too long after Sydney Pollack and Robert
Redford decided they wouldn't work together again
for a while, they got together to discuss an idea of
William Goldman's. It was a western called *Mr. Horn*
that Redford loved and wanted Pollack to direct. But
Pollack saw problems in the Goldman script and said
he couldn't begin filming for quite a while.

Pollack asked Redford when he'd begin filming *All
The President's Men,* which he had just bought the
rights to. Redford told him there were legal problems
with the *Washington Post* and that filming would be
delayed. As they were discussing their separate future
projects, Redford suddenly jumped up and said,
"Wait a minute, Pollack. I just read something the
other day. It's absolutely ready to go. It's bullshit but
it's the kind of picture we've always talked about
wanting to do where you don't have to worry about
the meaning of this and the meaning of that. It's a
popcorn movie, a thriller. You'll see when you read it,
it goes like the wind."

Pollack agreed with Redford's assessment of *Six
Days of the Condor,* a CIA novel by James Grady in
which an Agency reader is suddenly caught up in
inexplicable events that make him a fugitive from
everyone he thought he could trust. Redford and
Pollack decided to change the location from Washington, D.C. to New York City, and they began filming
there in October of 1974.

The fact that he was working with the same director
for the fourth time didn't bother Redford. "I used to
think that wasn't a good idea—that it was better to
work with as many directors as you could for variety
and educational reasons. Now I think you can do
better working with someone who knows your work as
an actor, especially if you tend to be on the subtle
side. Sydney understands me as well as any director
and is able to bring out certain things in me as an
actor that don't have to be talked about. It really has a
lot to do with familiarity."

Pollack agrees that their friendship makes their jobs
easier. "We didn't have to have long discussions. By
this time I could work with him in a kind of short-

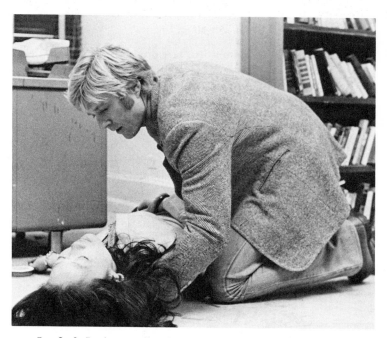

Joe finds Janice murdered

With Addison Powell

hand. I sometimes literally don't say a word and he knows exactly what I mean. Sometimes he'll do a take and I'll see him catch the corner of my eye and he'll see a little hesitation there and he'll say, 'O.K., once more.' "

Three Days of the Condor was "the least incident-filled film we ever did," says Pollack. But there were problems. Despite the fact that Redford had thought the book gave them a movie "absolutely ready to go," there were second thoughts once the project was underway. "We started to rewrite it," says Pollack, "and we brought in the same guy, David Rayfiel, who worked with us on *Jeremiah* and *The Way We Were.* He finally gets credit on this film. I think he helped turn it from a very good thriller into a very classy thriller."

The rewrite also helped to better define the character of Kathy, played by Faye Dunaway, "She's a more interesting woman in the movie than she was in the book" says Redford, "and the credit for that goes to Rayfiel and Sydney. It was their idea to make her a Diane Arbus-type photographer who takes lonely,

barren pictures of empty park benches and trees without leaves on them. Sydney is a very melancholy director, and his work reflects that. He likes to really explore the inner workings of a character."

One of the concerns of Redford and Pollack was how to integrate the love story with the fast-paced action of the film. "It was a very tricky thing to pull off," says Redford. "There's that old theory that you stop the action with a relationship in a thriller, and you risk losing the audience. But I think it worked in this film."

Redford did not find it easy to work with Faye Dunaway. He tells the story of being asked his opinion of Dunaway by a reporter on the set. "It was a difficult question because working with her was extremely difficult. I liked her enormously, but she's very difficult to work with. She's troubled—she's somewhere else. And I was trying to think of something that would get across my regard for her as a person and not get into critical analysis of the work.

"So I thought and thought and thought and I could sum up what I thought in two words. She had woman weight. It's an abstraction but that's the way it is. She has tremendous weight on the screen—good female weight. She's a real woman and she projects that and I think that's a virtue. When I said it I was told, 'Jesus, you can't say that! *Woman weight?* It sounds like she's fat . . .' and I said, 'No, that's not what I mean. If no one gets it, too bad.' Well, I was talked out of it in favor of something innocuous like 'real pro, fun to work with', shit like that. I'm not sure people ever really say what they mean."

During the filming of *Three Days*, Redford's next project, *All The President's Men,* occupied a good deal of his time. Having bought the rights to the book, Redford was the film's producer and was also working on the script with William Goldman. Reports emanated from the *Condor* set that Redford was spreading himself too thin, not devoting enough of his attention to the project at hand, and that Pollack was getting "pissed off" at him.

" 'Pissed off' isn't exactly the right way to describe it," says Pollack. "It's one thing to be angry at somebody and not sympathetic. Redford's too good a friend for that. It's another thing to be selfishly angry but totally understand, which I did. I'd tell him, 'Look, Redford, what are you doing?' But I was telling him as much for him as for me. His attention was being split between—never mind these two projects —all kinds of political speeches he had to make, the problems of the business merger at Sundance. He was constantly on the phone. Everybody wanted a piece of him. The fact is that it took a lot more work for me to get the work done with him."

Pollack doesn't think Redford's performance in *Three Days of the Condor* suffered because of his divided attention. "The only thing it did was frustrate me in trying to *get* his attention. I'd say, 'I'm trying to talk to you,' that sort of thing. But once he starts acting, he does what he has to do and he's good at it."

During the filming, revelations were coming out of Washington almost daily about covert operations of the CIA, including illegal surveillance and political assassinations. Suddenly, the bizarre, convoluted plot of *Three Days of the Condor* was believable. On one occasion, Richard Helms, the CIA director embroiled in the controversy, visited the set and chatted with Redford. "Are you having as much difficulty as I am?" he asked.

As the CIA news continued to make big headlines, anticipation of the release of *Condor* grew. Many were expecting a picture enlightening the populace about the hidden dangers of a secret intelligence organization in the United States. Once the film opened, however, it was clear that, although the revelations had helped the plot's credibility, the film was, as Redford had first described it, "a good popcorn thriller" and nothing more.

REVIEWS

"A tightly constructed, marvelously timely movie, *Three Days of the Condor* is a thinking man's horror film that details the ruthlessness and heartlessness of a quasi-incestuous CIA in blazing sequences of violence and terror. This film goes off like a rocket and stays high in the stratosphere of excitement until the suspense (which never flags) becomes almost unbearable. It is not only Sydney Pollack's direction and the taut screenplay that are responsible for the outstanding values of this splendid film. Robert Redford . . . gives one of the finest characterizations of his career, and Cliff Robertson, as a CIA official whose mind has been hand-tailored by the work he does, turns in a compelling performance full of style. Faye Dunaway is gracefully feminine and passionately strong . . ."

NORMA McLAIN STOOP,
After Dark

"*Three Days of the Condor* is idiotic drivel dedicated to the theory that gullible moviegoers will believe anything as long as it masquerades as a CIA expose. . . . The point of the movie is that you can't trust anybody in Washington, and if you believe one word of this hokum you'll also believe I have this perfectly splendid, slightly used bridge in Brooklyn I can sell you cheap."

REX REED

"A year ago we might have dismissed the bizarre plot of *Three Days of the Condor* as being ridiculously far-fetched. Today, after the disturbing revelations of recent months, nothing seems beyond the capabilities or power of the CIA. And so, we find ourselves accepting—willingly—most of what goes on in this movie . . . There is a chilling sense of reality to it all, and Sydney Pollack creates such an atmosphere of dread and danger that his film remains convincing enough to support our worst fears about CIA activity.

"Interestingly, Redford has never seemed better. One often feels that his approach to acting is too intellectual—he seems so remote and cold on the screen—but here, looking haggard and tense (and thoroughly deglamorized), he brings an awful loneliness, even a vulnerability, to the role."

KATHLEEN CARROLL,
New York Daily News

In the midst of terror, Joe and Kathy find time for romance

With Cliff Robertson

Pursuer and pursued meet in an elevator (with Max Von Sydow)

Director Pollack maps out a scene with Redford

223

"The film starts out well, but after the first few minutes you'd have to be one of those CIA readers to figure out what's going on. A Saturday-night drunk could walk blindfolded through a maze a lot easier than he could follow a plot like this one."

JOHN BARBOUR,
Los Angeles Magazine

"Wire-framed glasses, jeans and a stubble of beard aren't enough to make Redford totally convincing as a rather passive, bookish character who works with computers, but that reservation aside, *Condor* is easily Redford's most rewarding role since *The Candidate* three years ago. The shellacked smugness of his Gatsby, Waldo Pepper and teamings with Newman and Streisand has given way to an attractive skepticism and a more direct, less coy awareness of his appeal . . .

Much credit must also go to Faye Dunaway, who has become a first-rate actress after a bumpy post-*Bonnie and Clyde* period. In purely physical terms, actresses playing opposite Redford are generally given a tough deal, but Dunaway more than holds her own.

"*Three Days of the Condor* is too studious and monotoned to be a completely successful movie—it could certainly use a more creative directorial personality—but its contemporary subject, leading performances and appropriately paranoid point of view make it more than just a routine collection of murders and chases . . . One only wishes that Pollack and company would have let the larger implications speak for themselves and not put them in the mouths of the characters. There, they sound like speeches rather than truths."

MITCHELL S. COHEN
Brooklyn-Staten Island Good Times

Redford holds a press conference
during the filming

227

With Nicholas Coster

With Hoffman and director Alan Pakula

One of Woodward's sources insists on their meeting in an underground garage after Woodward takes two cabs. Dubbed "Deep Throat," the man is an insider who steers Woodward in the right direction with the least possible information.

Doggedly tracking down the story against many odds, the two reporters and their editors realize that the Watergate burglary was only a small fraction of a huge covert operation to sabotage the Democratic election effort, to use the FBI and CIA for improper activities and to gather millions of dollars in illegal campaign contributions for the re-election of President Richard Nixon. And as their investigation continues, they realize that the operation reaches into the highest level of the White House.

The White House continually denies the allegations and when a story by the two reporters is proven wrong, their investigation receives a severe setback. But the Post *stands by its reporters and more information is uncovered.*

Richard Nixon is re-elected by a landslide. But several months after he is inaugurated, the Woodward-Bernstein investigation has led to Congressional inquiries and high level resignations. In the ensuing months, many members of the government are indicted, and the House Judiciary Committee passes three articles of impeachment against President Nixon. Two years after the Woodward and Bernstein investigation began, Richard Nixon resigns the Presidency.

During Redford's "whistle stop" campaign through Florida to publicize *The Candidate* in June of 1972, five men were apprehended breaking into the Democratic National Headquaters at the Watergate Complex in Washington, D.C. The newsmen along for the tour began discussing the case with Redford, and their cynicism appalled him. "They said it was simply a matter of business as usual in Washington," he says. "They believed the truth about Watergate—and a lot of other things—would never come to light."

Redford was equally impressed, however, with the apparently dogged perseverence of two *Washington Post* reporters who were assigned to the case. And he was intrigued by them personally, by the differences that made them something of an odd couple: Bob Woodward, a WASP—cool, controlled and aristocratic; Carl Bernstein—a Jew, volatile and street-wise. "That was the first time I saw a potential film," says Redford. "I remember thinking, This is very interesting, a study in opposing characters and how they work together."

Long before Watergate became the political scandal of the century and toppled the administration of Richard Nixon, Redford decided to make a film about these two young reporters. "I'm interested in 'how to' movies—how to be a ski champion, how to run for office, how to run a newspaper. If you can inform people and entertain them at the same time, that to me is the best kind of movie."

Redford was also fascinated by the workings of reporters' minds. "I've always been on the other side," he says. "It was a double-edged sword for me. I'd seen myself criticized unfairly, misquoted, accused of things that weren't true and at times downright slandered by the press. On the other hand I'd often been unduly praised and blown up to gigantic proportions, equally unjustified. So I was fascinated by this monster. I wanted to find out what caused such inaccuracy and lack of perception by something that was supposed to be in the accuracy and perception business."

Redford got in touch with Woodward and told him he was interested in doing a film about the two reporters. Woodward replied, "Look, we're writing a book—maybe you should see the book when we're done. It's about Gordon Liddy, Howard Hunt and John Mitchell—what these three and some others did in connection with Watergate and the concealment." Redford volunteered his opinion that the story of how Woodward and his partner cracked the case would make far more interesting reading, and Woodward was intrigued.

Bernstein, however, doubted that anyone would be interested in "how they did it" and feared it would be construed as an ego trip. But once the team got into writing, Redford's suggestion helped solve a major problem. "The material was so bizarre and complicated," says Woodward, "that it needed a story line, and the reporters could give it that story line. Redford was a factor in getting us to write the kind of book we wrote."

Redford bought the rights to the book before it was written, paying $450,000. That turned out to be something of a bargain because, upon its publication early in 1974, the book, called *All The President's Men*, quickly became Number One on bestseller lists across the country.

While the book was being written, Redford began to hang around the *Washington Post* and its two star reporters, soaking up atmosphere and learning the day-to-day workings of a major newspaper. "It was an education for me," says Redford. "I've learned much more researching movies than I ever learned in school."

By this time Redford, who was producing the film along with Walter Coblenz, had begun to assemble a cast and crew for the film. His choice to play Bernstein was Dustin Hoffman, who physically resembled the reporter and who had tried to acquire film rights to the book himself. When Redford called Hoffman and asked him if he was interested, Hoffman replied, "I thought you'd never ask."

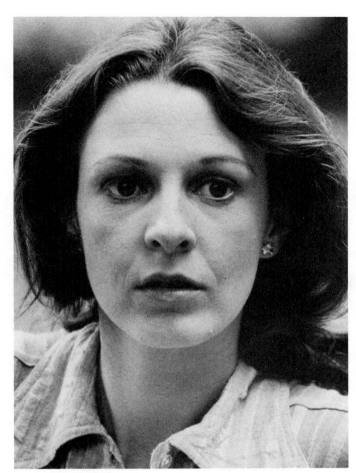

Jane Alexander

With Dustin Hoffman

Redford wasn't really all that interested in playing Woodward. "The role is certainly not illustrious or revelatory or scintillating," he says. "It's kind of a dogged, concentrated plodding character. But I wanted to do the project and playing the role was a sacrificial thing to get it going." It's no secret in Hollywood, of course, that it is far easier to get financial backing for a movie if it stars Robert Redford. Redford was more interested in playing the role Jack Nicholson eventually took in *One Flew Over The Cuckoo's Nest*—"a good acting role"—but turned it down because his total commitment to *President's Men* left him no time for anything else.

Redford's next concern was getting a director who would be "sympathetic" to his vision of the kind of movie *All The President's Men* should be. "I had a very strong, hard opinion of what it should look like and be like—almost to the point of directing it myself," he says. He decided not to—realizing, with the help of family, friends and co-workers, that that would be spreading himself too thin. Several directors were considered—among them Elia Kazan, Arthur Penn and Joseph Mankiewicz. But Redford was particularly interested in Alan Pakula, who had produced *Inside Daisy Clover*, because of his direction of the Oscar-winning film *Klute*. Redford had read that script and had not been very excited by it, but discovered an entirely different dimension in the finished film, created by Pakula's directorial evocation of fear and menace. Redford wanted that kind of suspense in *All The President's Men*, a suspense which was missing in the story since we had all lived through the ending.

Another difficult task in turning *All The President's Men* into cinema was the screenwriting, and Redford entrusted long-time collaborator William Goldman with the assignment. It proved tough even for an Oscar-winning pro like Goldman. He impressively solved the narrative problems created by the book's style, but his decision to make the movie a study in camaraderie between Bernstein and Woodward was universally disfavored. The big joke around the *Post* newsroom was that the movie should be called *Butch and Sundance Bring Down The Government.* Bernstein complained that the script read like a Henny Youngman joke book. Few at the *Post*, especially Executive Editor Ben Bradlee, were laughing.

Redford needed the *Post's* cooperation if *All The President's Men* were to be made at all. Bradlee, after reading Goldman's first script, nearly backed out of the project. He feared that he and the *Post* staff would be held up to ridicule. "Just remember pal," he told Redford bluntly, "that you go off and ride a horse or jump in the sack with some good–looking woman in your next film—but I am forever an asshole."

Redford tried to patch things up by explaining that he too was unhappy with the script and that it was a first draft. He felt it lacked details about the thing that interested him the most—the newsgathering process. He also felt that the relationship between the two reporters should be minimized, that the subject should be treated in a semi-documentary way. Goldman began to rework the script, and he and Redford told Bernstein and Woodward that comments and suggestions would be appreciated. "Movies are basically a collaborative art," says Goldman, who welcomed the reporters' help. "If you can't accept that, you don't belong in the business."

But neither Redford nor Goldman was quite prepared for the "comments and suggestions" which were soon to come from Carl Bernstein. At a meeting in Redford's New York apartment, Bernstein presented Redford with a completely rewritten script that he and girlfriend Nora Ephron had worked up. Woodward was embarrassed, and Goldman was nonplussed. Redford was somewhat amused: the script depicted Woodward as a plodding, dull worshipper of Bernstein, while Bernstein came off as a brilliant, incisive, womanizing hero. Redford's dry comment was, "Carl, Errol Flynn is dead."

The final script was a combination of input from everyone involved, plus a great deal of improvisation by the actors and director on the set.

Pakula, Redford and cinematographer Gordon Willis had originally hoped to film in the *Post's* gleaming, fluorescent-lighted newsroom, but that turned out to be impossible because it would have seriously impeded the newspaper's business. So set

(Opposite page) The cast and director of *All The President's Men* outside the *Washington Post* building. (Redford, Jason Robards, Jack Warden, Dustin Hoffman, Alan J. Pakula, Martin Balsam)

designer George Jenkins was called in to recreate the room on Warner Bros.' Burbank, California lot. No expense was spared, no detail overlooked. Jenkins measured every room, every desk. He placed everything where it was in the actual newsroom, even down to 1972 phonebooks and "Go, Redskins!" bumper stickers on desks. The *Post's* trash was shipped from Washington to fill wastepaper baskets. The *Post* reprinted hundreds of front pages from 1972 so that, for whatever day being represented in the film, the correct newspaper could be lying around the office.

Once filming got under way, Redford and Pakula's working relationship was a good one, but not without friction. "I knew there would be clashes," says Redford, "and there were some. But we basically agreed on what kind of film we wanted." Redford's recurring problem with conflicting working methods was compounded on this film because both Hoffman and Pakula like to discuss a scene at length, and Pakula prefers dozens of retakes, so he can have the widest possible choice in the cutting room. "Dustin is very

much like Barbra Streisand," Redford says. "He likes to talk everything to death. I'd always be thinking, Let's get it over with!"

There was, however, a great deal of mutual respect between the two stars. Hoffman says, "As an actor, Redford is wonderful fun to play against. Fast and very daring. If you stubbed your toe or dropped a pencil, he picked up on it right away and made it a part of the scene." Redford compliments Hoffman: "He's a fantastic actor. Working with him is like working with a stream of pure electricity. He's so intense and fluid you can't help but react."

By the time filming of *All The President's Men* was completed in November of 1975, Robert Redford had been involved with the project for almost three years. Involved in every facet of the production, he slept just four hours a night and seemed constantly on the move. "Part of me had to be the responsible producer," he says, "and part of me wanted to be creatively indulgent as an actor. These parts were always at war." The picture wound up thirty-five days over

(Top) With Jack Warden, Jason Robards and Dustin Hoffman

With Dustin Hoffman

Woodward and Bernstein fear they're being bugged

With Dustin Hoffman and Penny Fuller

schedule and $3.5 million over budget, costing nearly $8.5 million.

Redford was nervous about how the movie would be received. He was afraid that the American public wanted to forget Watergate and couldn't care less about Woodward and Bernstein. He asked everyone who saw advance screenings what they thought of it, and listened to their opinions. He eagerly attended sneak previews to get some idea of audience reaction. Finally, on April 8, 1976, the film opened, and all those involved with the film held their breath.

The film's reception was more than anyone anticipated. The critics seemed to be trying to outdo each other in praising the film, the direction, the script and the acting. John Simon, legendary for his lack of easy praise, wrote, *"All The President's Men* is worth seeing twice: once for everything about it and again just for the acting." Even more impressive than the critical acclaim were the box office receipts. The film made more than $7 million in its first seven days of release, more than *The Godfather* in a comparable period. The film, dubbed "the *Jaws* of the Potomac," became the cinematic event of the year and, it was suggested, was having an effect on the Presidential primaries in progress at the time. Redford's reaction? "I'm in a state of shock."

When there was criticism of the film, it centered on the semi-documentary quality of the script. Some viewers and critics felt that by sticking to the facts and devoting little cinematic time to insight into the personal relationship between the two reporters, Redford had made the film lifeless. Dustin Hoffman agrees with this assessment: "I told Bob he was drying the picture out. I said he should add a scene where Woodward and Bernstein were really having it out. But he didn't. I would have fought more, but by the time I saw the film it was too late to make the radical changes I wanted. In my opinion, the film is a little too smooth. I would have left a few hairs on the lens."

Redford doesn't think it would have worked as well that way. "Hype a picture like this," he says, "and you lose credibility. Story and atmosphere were the important things here. Character and relationships were less important. We decided that right at the beginning, and we stuck to our guns. I never worked on a picture that so much thought went into. A lot of it was preventative thought, not so much do this as don't do that. Don't make it a movie about Nixon or Watergate. Don't take a partisan position. Don't set out to celebrate the press. Don't be too impressed with the history involved. Don't fall in love with the *Washington Post.* Do make a movie about the press, about two reporters who did a difficult job of reporting and did it well."

Always his own toughest critic, Redford is happy

234

Redford meets with the real Bob Woodward to discuss the film.

with *All The President's Men*. "To an extent that surprises me," he says, "the movie I wanted to make is right up there on the screen: a movie about the truth, and how close we came to losing the right to know it."

REVIEWS

"*All The President's Men*, directed by Alan J. Pakula, written by William Goldman and largely pushed into being by the continuing interest of one of its stars, Robert Redford, is a lot of things all at once: a spellbinding detective story about the work of the two *Washington Post* reporters who helped break the Watergate scandal, a breathless adventure that recalls the triumphs of Frank and Joe Hardy in that long-ago series of boys' books, and a vivid footnote to some contemporary American history that still boggles the mind. The film is an unequivocal smash-hit — the thinking man's *Jaws*."

VINCENT CANBY,
The New York Times

"This film is a rare and classic example of what Hollywood can do when it's willing to bank on good taste, shrewd intelligence and deep personal conviction. Though not perfect, *All the President's Men* is an absolutely breathless entertainment, and it successfully carries the weight of history on its shoulders. It works as a detective thriller (even though everyone knows the ending), as a credible (if occasionally romanticized) primer on the prosaic fundamentals of big-league investigative journalism, and, best of all, as a chilling tone poem that conveys the texture of the terror in our nation's capital during that long night when an aspiring fascist regime held our democracy under siege."

FRANK RICH,
New York Post

"From Redford's thoughtful, self-effacing performance to Gordon Willis' telling photography (which jarringly contrasts the penetrating glare of the city room with the dark, threatening world outside), *All the President's Men* is a mentally absorbing, vitally important film. And thanks largely to the psychological insight of director Alan Pakula, it may well become an American film classic."

KATHLEEN CARROLL,
New York Daily News

"The one flaw is the film's end. After getting us involved with two reporters for over two years of time and two hours of film, and after leading us to expect to see actual news footage of Nixon's resignation, all we're shown is the teletype keys spelling it all out. And, what's worse, we see absolutely no reaction from the two reporters whose story may have caused it all.

"Other than that, *All the President's Men* is the kind of a film to make all of us feel the pride and pain that comes with having a free press."

JOHN BARBOUR,
Los Angeles Magazine

"Even if you are simply seeking entertainment, it will satisfy your needs and fulfill your stiffest demands. Written with craftsmanlike precision by William Goldman and directed with brilliance and cinematic skill by Alan Pakula, *All the President's Men* works on several levels. It contains every element of mystery, tension and suspense indigenous to a great detective story. That's pretty staggering, considering the control and dignity involved. Not one gun goes off, no bodies are slashed and there are no souped-up action sequences. Yet my heart pounded harder than it has in any saga I've seen in the past few years.

"Best of all, however, are Robert Redford and Dustin Hoffman, as the glue holding all the bits of paper together, and somehow they manage the impossible task of submerging their own superstar images to literally become the reporters they are playing. Redford's well-bred, Ivy League charm is used to good advantage as Woodward, while Hoffman's eager, rumpled, chain-smoking Bernstein is a perfect counterpart. As different as they are, they merge into one molecular structure in a powerful scene that gave me goosebumps."

REX REED

"Pakula's Washington, as photographed brilliantly by Gordon Willis, is divided into the dark world of the Watergate conspiracy and the forces of light, whose symbolic headquarters is the vast gleaming newsroom of the *Washington Post*. Here Redford and Hoffman bang away at their stories amid the televised faces of Richard Nixon and his aides. Pakula is driving home the point that at the heart of Watergate was a battle between opposing forces for the public consciousness."

JACK KROLL,
Newsweek

"Like the worst of the Bicentennial specials, *All the President's Men* is tedious and literal-minded; it diminishes the most dramatic story of the decade.

"The Woodward-Bernstein book worked as a first-rate detective story, but mystery stories are verbal rather than visual, and they often fail to make the transition from print to celluloid. On screen *All the President's Men* consists of 135 minutes of expository dialogue—telephone conversations and lengthy interview scenes in which characters regurgitate information that most of us already know. Alan J. Pakula, a competent but uninspired director, fails to supply the energy and narrative drive that Costa-Gavras brought to political thrillers like *Z* and *The Confession.*

"Robert Redford and Dustin Hoffman also give skillful performances, but they are hampered by the script; they have no characters to play. Good reporters combine stubbornness, idealism, ambition and ruthlessness; but the movie seems too frightened of offending Woodward and Bernstein to present them in the round. Sanitized and emasculated, the characters never come alive."

STEPHEN FARBER,
New West

"*All The President's Men* is such a model of efficient filmmaking that nothing that Alan J. Pakula has heretofore directed (including *Klute*) or that William Goldman has written (*Butch Cassidy and*

The Sundance Kid, The Great Waldo Pepper) could have prepared us for the success of this picture. *All The President's Men* is as remarkable for its understatement, for the clichés it avoids, for all of the things it doesn't do, as for the things that it does do.

"Chief among the latter is the manner in which it utilizes two fine actors, Robert Redford as Woodward and Dustin Hoffman as Bernstein, to tell us all that we need to know about two reporters whose private lives do not impinge on this film, even peripherally. *All The President's Men* is a portrait of life on a large metropolitan daily told entirely in terms of the investigation of a single event. The Bernstein-Woodward characters must emerge from their actions and reactions during this investigation, which means they are roles to which the actors must bring a great deal of baggage containing their own attitudes, insights and observations. They must play straight men to the action, and had they hammed it up at all, the film would have gone out the window."

ANTHONY ASTRACHAN
The New York Times (Sunday)

Woodward and Bernstein try to fit the pieces together

A CANDID GALLERY

Jeremiah Johnson

Redford participates in the re-burial of John Jeremiah Johnston, upon whose life the movie was based

Redford attends the Cannes Film Festival opening of *Jeremiah* with Lola and Sydney Pollack.

The Sting

Redford and Newman—together again for the first time

(Top) George Roy Hill and Redford during filming

Tell Them Willie Boy Is Here

With Katharine Ross during filming

Butch Cassidy
and the Sundance Kid

Lola, Jamie and Shauna visit Daddy
on the set

Lola and Bob attend the premiere of *Waldo Pepper*, a benefit for Lola's Consumer Action Now

(Top left) Posing for publicity portraits, Bob and Barbra give photographer Steve Schapiro a hard time

(Above) Filming the final scene

(Top right) Hubbell and Katie get married (a scene never used in the film)

The Great Gatsby

All The President's Men

Pakula, Hoffman and
Redford on location

Redford relaxes during a
filming hiatus

(Left) Redford and Farrow try to
keep warm as a scene is set up

A LOOK INTO THE FUTURE

Once *All The President's Men* opened in April of 1976, Robert Redford had been working steadily for more than five years, and had made nine movies in that time. His all-consuming involvement in *President's Men*, he said, had left him "numb." "I don't want to work for a while, not for at least a year. I'm not concerned with momentum. I do enough movies. I need some time to cool out and recharge."

Redford did agree, however, to a stint in the all-star cast of *A Bridge Too Far*. Redford got the producers to agree to film his segments in the Fall of 1976, so he could have the summer off with his family. His part would require perhaps three or four weeks of work and, it was reported, Redford was receiving $2 million. "They offered me so much money I'd be nuts to turn it down."

At this writing, Redford has no plans other than to "recharge" and work on the solar house he is building in Utah near his Sundance resort.

Possible future projects for Redford include *Mr. Horn*, the Western that William Goldman and Sydney Pollack have worked up for him, and a film about business. Redford has long said that he wanted to film a trilogy including an athlete, a politician and a businessman, and he has been reviewing several business-oriented scripts. He also wants to do another love story and another comedy, perhaps teaming again with Barbra Streisand or Jane Fonda.

Redford's production company, Wildwood, Inc., is becoming involved in more projects, and Redford's position as a producer seems secure. He may also turn to directing. "I'd like to direct," he says. "The little details would drive me crazy, but I'd let someone else handle those. What I would enjoy is visualizing a movie and seeing it turn out that way on the screen. That's when it's really fun."

Redford and director Richard Attenborough during filming

Redford in the Joseph E. Levine spectacular, *A Bridge Too Far*

A PORTRAIT GALLERY

Alfred Hitchcock Presents—"A Tangled Web" (1962)

Inside Daisy Clover (1965)

Tell Them Willie Boy Is here (1969)

The Chase (1965)

The Great Waldo Pepper (1974)